Classroom

Adobe® PageMill™ ^version 2.0

Library of Congress Catalog No.: 96-77655

ISBN: 1-56830-319-X

10 9 8 7 6 5 4 3 2 First Printing: April 1997

Published by Adobe Press, Adobe Systems Incorporated, San Jose, California. For information on becoming an Adobe Certified Expert (ACE) with Adobe PageMill, send an e-mail to certification@adobe.com or visit the Adobe World Wide Web site (http://www.adobe.com).

Direct to plate prepress and printing by GAC Shepard Poorman, Indianapolis, Indiana. Printed in the United States of America.

Published simultaneously in Canada.

Adobe Press books are published and distributed by Macmillan Computer Publishing USA. For individual, educational, corporate, or retail sales accounts, call 1-800-428-5331, or 1-317-581-3500. For information on Adobe Press books, address Macmillan Computer Publishing USA, 201 West 103rd Street, Indianapolis, Indiana, 46290 or visit the Macmillan World Wide Web site (http://www.mcp.com/hayden/adobe).

Part number: 0397 2110 (4/97 MW)

Contents

Introduction

Adobe® PageMill™ is page-authoring software for the World Wide Web. With Adobe PageMill you can build and preview text, images, animation, sounds, tables, and links on a Web page. You can drag and drop images, multimedia objects, and links directly onto a Web page, and apply standard HTML formats and styles to text without typing HTML code.

Prerequisites

Before beginning to use *Adobe PageMill Classroom in a Book*, you should have a working knowledge of the Windows® or MacOS® operating conventions. In particular, you should know how to do the following:

- Use the mouse and standard menus and commands
- Open, save, and close files
- Resize application windows
- Position multiple windows on-screen
- Drag and drop files and objects from one window to another

If you need to review these techniques, see your Windows or MacOS documentation.

About Classroom in a Book™

Adobe PageMill Classroom in a Book teaches you the techniques that you need to get the most out of Adobe PageMill. The lessons in this book center on the creation of a World Wide Web site for a fictional arts school, the Art Academy. The Web site you'll assemble includes an introductory home page, an interactive fill-in form (both of these files you'll create from scratch), and a set of pages describing curriculum.

The pages link together as you would expect in a Web site, and the links include ones to downloadable files (an admissions application and an invitation to a show of student work) and actual pages on the World Wide Web (including the Adobe Systems Incorporated home page). Although you do not actually go through the steps of uploading your completed files to a Web server for broadcast on the Web, you will open the Web site using your browser, previewing the site as it will appear when published.

Each lesson concludes with a review section summarizing what you've covered. Taking time to read the review sections will help you retain important concepts about the lesson and about PageMill.

System requirements

Adobe PageMill Classroom in a Book can be used on a computer that runs Windows, Windows NT, or MacOS. In addition to the system requirements for the system you use, you need the Adobe PageMill 2.0 program and a CD-ROM drive to use the *Adobe PageMill Classroom in a Book* files.

Windows system requirements

To complete the lessons in Windows, you need the following hardware and software:

- An 80486 (or faster) processor
- Microsoft Windows 95 or Windows NT 4.0
- 8 MB RAM for Windows 95, or 16 MB RAM for Windows NT
- 20 MB free hard-disk space
- VGA or better display
- A CD-ROM drive for installation
- Adobe Acrobat® Reader 3.0 (available on the Classroom in a Book CD-ROM in the Acroread folder)

• Netscape Navigator™ 3.0 or later, or Microsoft® Internet Explorer 3.0 or later (or an equivalent browser)

• QuickTime™ for Windows 2.1.2 (available on the PageMill 2.0 CD-ROM)

• MoviePlayer™ 2.1.2 (installed with QuickTime from the PageMill 2.0 CD-ROM)

MacOS system requirements

To complete the lessons in MacOS, you need the following hardware and software:

• System 7™ Pro or System 7.5 or later (to drag and drop files)

• 4 MB of free RAM (8-16 MB preferable)

• 20-40 MB free hard-disk space

• A CD-ROM drive for installation

• Adobe Acrobat Reader 3.0 (available on the Classroom in a Book CD-ROM in the Acroread folder)

• Netscape Navigator 3.0 or later, or Microsoft Internet Explorer 3.0 or later (or an equivalent browser)

• QuickTime 2.5 (available on the PageMill 2.0 CD-ROM)

• MoviePlayer 2.5 (installed with QuickTime from the PageMill 2.0 CD-ROM)

Getting started

Before you begin using the *Adobe PageMill Classroom in a Book*, you need to make sure you have installed the required software and files.

Installing other software

If you haven't already done so, install the Adobe PageMill 2.0 program. The user guide that comes with Adobe PageMill 2.0 includes complete instructions for installing Adobe PageMill.

Install a Web browser, such as Netscape Navigator 3.0 or Microsoft Internet Explorer 3.0. Note that the *Adobe PageMill Classroom in a Book* files have been tested only on those two browsers.

Install Adobe Acrobat Reader 3.0, which adds the PDFViewer plug-in required to view the PDF files included as part of the sample Art Academy Web site. To install Acrobat Reader, open the Acroread folder on the Classroom in a Book CD-ROM and double-click Setupex.exe (Windows—the extension may not be visible) or the Acrobat Reader icon (MacOS).

Note: *The PDFViewer plug-in is added automatically to the Web browser plug-ins folder if the browser is installed before you install Acrobat Reader 3.0. If you have multiple browsers installed on your system, or if you installed a browser after installing Acrobat Reader, the PDFViewer plug-in may not be in the correct folder. In that case, move a copy of Nppdf32.dll (Windows) or PDFViewer (MacOS) to the correct browser plug-ins folder.*

Finally, install QuickTime for Windows 2.1.2 or QuickTime 2.5 (MacOS), which also installs the Movie Player program. To install QuickTime, open the QuickTime folder on the PageMill 2.0 CD-ROM and double-click Qt32.exe (Windows) or the QuickTime icon (MacOS).

Copying the Classroom in a Book files

The Classroom in a Book CD-ROM includes folders with all the electronic files needed to complete the Classroom in a Book lessons. Each lesson has its own folder within the folder called WEBSITE. To use the files during the lessons, copy the WEBSITE folder from the Classroom in a Book CD-ROM to your hard disk. If you want to view the finished Web site, also copy the ACADEMY folder from the CD-ROM to your hard disk.

Note: *Since the files on the Classroom in a Book CD-ROM are not read-only (Windows) or locked (MacOS), it is possible to make and save changes to them after you have copied them to your system. If you make unwanted changes to a PageMill file on your system, choose Revert to Saved from the File menu to restore it. If you inadvertently save any changes to a file, you can recopy the file from the Classroom in a Book CD-ROM to view the original file.*

Setting PageMill preferences

Before you begin the first lesson, you need to set some PageMill Preferences to make sure that what you see on your screen matches the descriptions in each lesson.

1 Start PageMill.

2 Choose Edit > Preferences.

3 In Windows, click the General tab. In MacOS, click the General icon from the list of icons on the left.

4 In MacOS only, select the first option in the Tiling section, which lines up tiled windows side by side on-screen.

Note: In Windows, the tiling option is not a preference setting. Tiling options are available from the Window menu.

5 In the Browsing section, choose Preview Mode for Open Pages In. Also choose Same Window for Local Links.

6 In the Browsing section in Windows, click the Browse button next to Open Remote Links Using, locate a Web browser on the hard disk, and click Open. In MacOS, choose Select Browser from the Remote Links menu, locate a Web browser on the hard disk, and click Open.

7 In Windows, click the Page tab. In MacOS, click the Page icon from the list of icons on the left.

8 Leave the options in the Appearance section set to Default.

9 In the File Format section, leave the Line Breaks and Suffix options set to their default values, unless you plan to upload the Art Academy Web site to a Web server. In that case, choose from the following options:

• Set the Line Breaks to match the Web server's platform. For example, choose DOS if the Web server runs Windows 95 or Windows NT.

• Set the Suffix to match the file naming conventions of the Web server. For example, choose .HTM if uploading to a DOS server or if working on a DOS machine. Note that the Classroom in a Book files all use the .HTM extension (suffix). If you plan to upload the sample Art Academy Web site to a Web server, make sure your Web server supports .HTM extensions.

10 In Windows, click the Switch To tab. In MacOS, scroll down to the Switch To icon on the left and click it.

11 In Windows, click the Add button in the Switch To Menu Applications section, locate a Web browser on your hard disk, and click Open. In MacOS, click the small application icon, locate a Web browser on your hard disk, and click Open.

MacOS Note: If a Web browser is already installed, the browser name will appear in the Switch To Menu Applications section and you can skip step 11.

12 Leave the rest of the preferences set to their default values and click OK to close the Preferences dialog box.

Now you're ready to begin the first lesson.

Other resources

Adobe PageMill Classroom in a Book is not meant to replace documentation that comes with Adobe PageMill. Only the commands and options used in the lessons are explained in this book. For comprehensive information about all the program's features, refer to the *Adobe PageMill 2.0 User Guide.*

More information about Adobe products and services is available from the following sources:

• Forums on CompuServe® (GO ADOBEAPP) and America Online℠ (keyword: Adobe); forums and availability may vary by country

• The Adobe home page on the World Wide Web (http://www.adobe.com)

• Adobe's own technical support bulletin board system (206-623-6984)

• FaxYI, a free fax-based service that provides the latest technical information about Adobe products (206-628-5737)

• The Adobe Certification Expert™ (ACE) program; send e-mail to: certification@adobe.com

Lesson 1

Creating the Home Page

If you've followed the installation procedures and set preferences as described in the introduction, you are ready to begin creating the Art Academy Web site.

Although many of the Web site pages in this Classroom in a Book are already partially completed, you'll create the first page—typically called a Home page—from scratch. In the course of completing the lesson you'll learn how to:

• Create a new PageMill file

• Specify a page title

• Use HTML heading levels to format text

• Add and resize images

• Duplicate objects

• Apply custom colors to text and to the page background

Starting the Home page

You can open existing HTML documents or create them from scratch. In this lesson, you'll start from scratch to see how quickly and easily you create an effective page.

Depending on the platform, start the Adobe PageMill 2.0 application as follows:

• In Windows, choose Start > Programs > Adobe > PageMill 2.0 > Adobe PageMill 2.0.

• In MacOS, open the Adobe PageMill 2.0 folder and double-click the Adobe PageMill 2.0 icon.

A new untitled window appears.

You'll start creating the Home page on the untitled empty page.

First, notice the toolbar at the top of the window. As you slowly move your cursor across the buttons, text that identifies each button appears either next to the button (Windows) or on the right (MacOS). Note, too, that two rows of buttons on the right are not yet active. The top row is active when you select an image, and the bottom row is active when you are creating tables. You'll get to both in later lessons.

In Windows only, if you cannot see all the image and table buttons on the right side of the toolbar, then the parent window—where the menu commands are located—may be too small. To enlarge the window, drag its bottom right corner out, then maximize the Untitled window, if necessary.

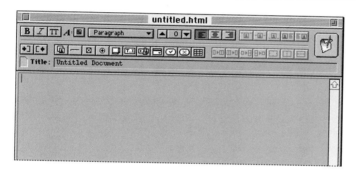

Saving, naming, and titling documents

First, you'll save and name the Home page file, and also give the page a title. A page title is displayed when a page is opened in a Web browser. The title is also used for bookmarks in a browser.

1 Choose File > Save Page As.

2 Open the Lesson1 folder in the WEBSITE folder on your hard drive.

3 In the dialog box, type **HOME.HTM** in uppercase letters for the filename.

UNIX® Web servers are case sensitive, and most Web servers are UNIX, so be sure to type the filename exactly as shown. In a Web site, files and links to those files must be named exactly the same, including upper- and lowercase letters. Otherwise, the Web server won't be able to find the file and display it.

4 Click Save to save the document and return to the document window.

The page you have created now has a filename. When you set preferences in the introduction, you specified that the filename use the .HTM extension. For a Web browser to recognize a file as one that contains HTML code, the file must use either the .HTM or .HTML extension.

In PageMill, the filename always appears in the title bar of the window. In a Web browser, the title bar can display either the filename or a title you specify (the filename is the default title).

Often, you will want to give the page a title that's different (or that provides more information) than the filename, so visitors to the Web site have an easy reference. The page title is also used by the Web browser when it displays a bookmark, or a list of pages the user has visited, which is sometimes called a History list.

You type the title of the page below the toolbar, in the Title text box.

5 In the Title box below the toolbar, select the text "Untitled Document."

6 Type **The Art Academy Home Page,** then press Enter (Windows) or Return (MacOS) to store the title in the page.

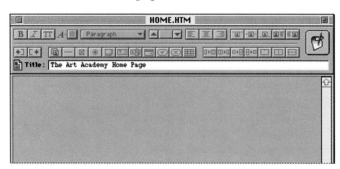

You'll see how the page title is displayed when you view the Home page in the Web browser at the end of this lesson.

Typing and formatting text

You'll start the Home page by typing the introductory text, the titles of the main sections of the Web site, and then the standard copyright information.

As you go, you'll also apply paragraph attributes similar to those in other software applications, as well as formats specific to the HTML standard.

1 With the insertion point at the top of the page, type (in capital letters) W E L C O M E, leaving a space between each letter for emphasis.

2 In the toolbar, click the Center Align Text button (≡).

The paragraph moves to the center of the window.

Because each Web browser displays text according to the font, size, and color specified by the user, text is specified as a particular HTML format (a heading, for example) rather than individually styled and sized.

HTML formats are like paragraph styles in word-processing or desktop publishing applications, except that you cannot modify them. The formats specify relative sizes and formatting, but are styled with the specific fonts, sizes, and colors that the user chooses in the Web browser preferences.

3 Now click an insertion point anywhere in the text "WELCOME" and choose Format > Heading > Largest.

When displayed in a Web browser, the WELCOME text will be formatted at a specific size determined by the user's preference, but it will always be larger than other text on the page.

Adding horizontal rules

Before you type the next section of the Home page, you'll add a line, called a horizontal rule, as a design element to help define the section.

1 Click an insertion point to the right of the word "WELCOME" and press Enter or Return.

This creates a paragraph in which you can position the horizontal rule.

2 In the toolbar, click the Insert Horizontal Rule button (—).

The rule appears in the paragraph.

By default, the rule extends the width of the window. Now you'll change the thickness of the rule.

3 Press Enter or Return so that a new paragraph appears below the rule.

4 Move the cursor over the rule, and when the cursor changes to a pointer, click the rule to select it.

When you select a graphic object in PageMill, selection handles appear on the bottom and right sides of the object allowing you to resize it vertically, horizontally, or (by dragging the corner handle) both vertically and horizontally in one action.

5 Select the handle centered on the bottom of the rule, and drag down about one-quarter of an inch.

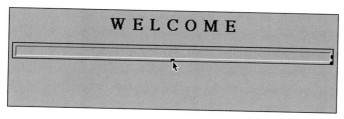

6 Release the mouse button and click below the rule to deselect it. The rule is now thicker.

Now you'll create a new section of the page, and then you'll save the work so far.

7 If the insertion point is not in the center of the screen below the rule, click below the rule to place it there.

8 Choose Format > Heading > Large.

Next, you'll create a navigation bar by typing the names of the four main sections of the Web site and enclosing each name in brackets. The text is a little more legible if you add a space after each opening bracket ([) and before each closing bracket (]).

9 Type [**Academic Offerings**] [**Admissions**] [**Tour**] [**Events**].

10 Press Enter or Return to create an empty paragraph, then choose File > Save Page.

 To save a page, use the shortcut Ctrl+S (Windows) or Command+S (MacOS).

Later you'll link each word to the part of the Web site it refers to, so that the line becomes what is called a navigation bar. The brackets separate the text, so it's easier to see the hot spots in the navigation bar.

All that's needed at this point is another rule below the line so that the navigation bar occupies its own section of the page. You'll add the rule using a different technique than you used to create the first one. Rather than insert a new rule, you'll make an exact duplicate of the first one, and position the duplicate below the line of text you just typed. This ensures that the two rules are the exact same height and width.

11 Select the rule you added earlier by clicking on it. (Do not select the resize handles on the rule.)

12 Hold down Ctrl (Windows) or Option (MacOS) and drag down past the last line of text (the navigation bar). When the insertion point appears in an empty paragraph, release the mouse button.

The new horizontal rule appears.

You could have used the Copy and Paste commands in the Edit menu to accomplish the same task, but the drag-and-drop technique is faster.

The only change to make now is to specify an equal amount of space above and below the line of type that appears between the rules. Since the paragraph format controls the vertical spacing between paragraphs and graphic objects, you'll simply apply the same paragraph format to both rules.

13 Click the topmost rule to select it, and choose Format > Heading > Large.

The navigation bar is vertically centered between the rules.

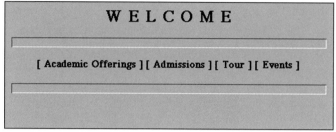

Typing and formatting a footer

For most Web sites, it's important to have a footer on the Home page (if not on every page) that describes basic information about the site, including legal status, the date it was last updated, and so on. You'll add a brief footer to the Art Academy Home page.

1 Click an insertion point at the right edge of the bottom rule, and press Enter or Return to create a new paragraph below the rule.

2 Click the Left Align Text button (≡) in the toolbar.

3 Type **Copyright 1997 by the Art Academy. All Rights Reserved.** When you finish typing, leave the insertion point to the right of the word "Reserved."

On a Web page, footer information is often displayed in italics, to set it off from the rest of the page. You can use the PageMill format called Address to quickly style text this way.

4 Choose Format > Address, then press Enter or Return.

5 In the new paragraph, type the following: **Comments or Questions? Contact: Webmaster@Artacad.edu.**

In Lesson 7 you'll come back to this footer and learn how to make the electronic mail address a special kind of link—one that a visitor to the Web site can click to send e-mail to the Art Academy over the Internet.

6 Choose File > Save Page.

Inserting and modifying images

With the text pretty much complete, you can now add images to make the page more appealing. Images are perhaps the most important design elements on Web pages; not only do they attract attention and give your pages a personal style, but they help break up blocks of text that can be difficult to read on-screen without visual variety.

PageMill lets you work with the universally supported GIF (Graphics Interchange Format) file type and also with JPEG (Joint Photographic Experts Group) images (though not all browsers can display them). You can also use PICT graphics, a graphics file defined with the Apple® QuickDraw™ screen description language, but PICT files work a little differently. When you import a PICT file, PageMill duplicates it in the PageMill Resources folder and converts the duplicate to the GIF file type. Almost all illustration or image-editing software applications can save or export artwork or photographs in GIF or JPEG format.

Images can help make up for the limited typographic effects of HTML. You'll notice that the images you place in this lesson include well-designed type that adds flair and distinction to the page. The images were also built for speed so that the image data would download in a reasonable amount of time, even if a visitor to the Web site used a slower modem to connect to the Internet.

Inserting an image

There's more than one way to bring an image into the active document. You'll learn the two most common methods in this section: using the Place Object button in the toolbar and dragging a file from a folder. First you'll use the Place Object button.

1 Click to the left of the word "WELCOME" in the paragraph at the top of the page, and press Enter or Return.

This creates an empty paragraph into which you'll add the image. As with horizontal rules, images always reside in an existing paragraph.

2 Click in the empty paragraph at the top of the page, and then click the Place Object button (▣) in the toolbar.

3 In the dialog box, open the Images folder within the Lesson1 folder within the WEBSITE folder.

4 Select HOMELOGO.GIF and then click Place.

The image appears at the size at which it was created in Adobe Photoshop®.

Resizing an image

Although PageMill lets you resize an image to any size, you should resize only to make small adjustments. Resizing large amounts can distort the image or significantly change its resolution. In general, you should create images at the size you'll need on the Web page.

You'll adjust the image you just placed by a small amount.

1 Scroll, if necessary, to bring the right edge of the image into view, then click the image to select it.

The three resize handles appear.

2 Press Shift and drag the handle at the lower-right corner up and to the left toward the center of the image, until the image is about a half-inch narrower.

The image resizes proportionally as long as you hold down the Shift key.

3 Release the mouse button.

Inserting the navigation button

Now you'll insert an image by dragging it to the page from a folder. You'll start by creating a new section of the page, again reusing a horizontal rule to define the section.

1 Click an insertion point to the right of the bottom rule, and press Enter or Return to create a paragraph for the new image.

Since you are about to switch from the PageMill application to Explorer (Windows) or the Finder (MacOS), this is a good time to save.

2 Choose File > Save Page.

3 In Windows, click the Start button in the taskbar, and then choose Programs > Windows Explorer. In MacOS, choose Finder from the Application menu in the upper-right corner of the screen.

4 Locate and open the WEBSITE folder, then choose View > List (Windows) or View > By Name (MacOS), if necessary.

5 Open the Lesson1 folder, then open the Images folder to display the folder contents.

Windows   *MacOS*

To drag and drop from Explorer (Windows) or the Finder (MacOS), you must make sure that the file you need and the destination window are both clearly visible on-screen.

6 If necessary, move and resize the HOME.HTM window and the WEBSITE folder window so that you can view them simultaneously.

7 Drag the WHATSNEW.GIF file from the Images folder to the HOME.HTM window, and release the mouse button when the insertion point appears in the paragraph you created for the image.

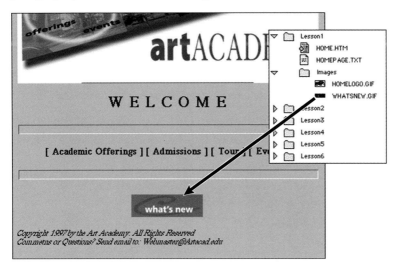

8 Click the HOME.HTM window to make it active. With the image selected, click the Left Align Object button (⊏◆) in the toolbar.

9 Choose File > Save Page.

Reusing text from other applications

You just dragged an image from a folder, but you can also drag text onto a page in PageMill. The ability to copy text from another application makes it easy to create your text in a word-processing application, for example, and bring it into your Web pages when the text is complete. In this section you'll reuse text that has already been typed into a text file.

Note: In Windows, dragging and dropping text between PageMill and other applications or the desktop requires using WordPad or Word. Notepad does not support the drag-and-drop technique. In MacOS, you must have Apple System 7 Pro or System 7.5 or later installed on your system.

1 To create a line for the paragraph you are about to add to the page, click to the right of the word "WELCOME" and press Enter or Return.

2 In Windows, click the Explorer window to make it active. In MacOS, use the Application menu to return to the Finder.

3 Make sure the contents of the Lesson1 folder are visible, then open the text file as follows, depending on the platform:

• In Windows, start the WordPad or Word program, then open the file called HOMEPAGE.TXT in the Lesson1 folder. To make the file available, you may need to choose All Documents (*.*) for Files of Type. In WordPad, you may want to wrap the text so you can view all of it inside the window. Choose View > Options, then click the Text tab and select Wrap to Window. Click OK.

• In MacOS, double-click the HOMEPAGE.TXT file. The file opens in SimpleText.

The file contains text that you can add to the Home page.

The Art Academy fosters experimentation and exploration. By providing exceptional instructors and specialized facilities, the Academy creates a stimulating environment that encourages students to find their individual artistic styles.

Text file

4 Move and resize the text window to the right so that the HOME.HTM window is clearly visible.

5 Select the text in the text file.

6 Drag the selected paragraph from the text window to the HOME.HTM window. When the insertion point appears in the paragraph below the word "WELCOME," release the mouse button.

The paragraph appears in the HOME.HTM window. Because inserted text uses the format of the preceding paragraph, the paragraph is styled as Largest Heading. You'll need to make it smaller.

7 Click in the HOME.HTM window to make it active and, with the paragraph still selected, choose Format > Paragraph so that text entered into this paragraph will have the correct format applied.

8 With the paragraph still selected, choose Format > Indent Right.

The Indent Right command actually moves the selected paragraph inward from the left and right edges of the document window. Since this decreases the length of lines in the paragraph, it increases readability.

9 With the HOME.HTM window active, choose File > Save Page.

10 Quit the word processor.

Using the Inspector to set text and background colors

The final design enhancement you'll make to the Home page is to set a new background color and a new text color.

1 If the Inspector isn't visible, choose View > Show Inspector (Windows) or Window > Show Inspector (MacOS).

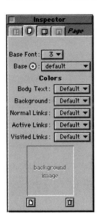

This palette is divided into four tabs, which are activated only when the appropriate elements on the page are selected. Each tab provides controls for these elements:

⊞ The Frame tab provides controls for adjusting frames. You'll learn about frames in Lesson 5.

▯ The Page tab provides page controls for the base font size, colors, and the background image.

▭ The Form tab lets you specify a Common Gateway Interface (CGI) script for a specified form. You'll learn about forms in Lesson 6.

▣ The Object tab provides controls for adjusting attributes of an object, such as an image or table.

2 If necessary, click the Page tab (□) in the Inspector to display the settings that modify the active page.

3 Choose View > Show Color Panel (Windows) or Window > Show Color Panel (MacOS) to display the Color Panel, a color palette that lets you assign colors to various page elements. You'll use it to assign a color to the page background, which is gray by default.

4 In the Color Panel, select the white color (at the top of the first column) and drag the circle onto the Background menu in the Inspector.

If you inadvertently drag the color to the wrong menu, choose Edit > Undo (Windows) or Edit > Undo Background Color (MacOS) and repeat the step.

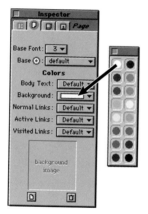

The background of the page is now the color you just selected. Note how the lighting and shadows have changed for the two rules. The color is also displayed in the Background menu.

It's best to set the page background first, so that you can more easily pick a text color that's clearly legible against the background. Now you'll pick a text color. This time, you'll define a custom color.

5 In the Inspector, choose Custom for Body Text.

The Color dialog box (Windows) or Apple Color Picker dialog box (MacOS) appears.

6 In the dialog box, select a blue-green color that matches the text in the Art Academy logo at the top of the page.

7 Click OK to close the dialog box.

The text on the page changes to the color you specified. The custom color appears in the Body Text section of the Inspector. Remember that the text color setting applies to all the text on the page, not to selected text, and not to text on any other page.

8 Choose File > Save Page.

The Home page is now complete.

Viewing source code

In case you're wondering exactly how much HTML code PageMill automatically generated for you, PageMill allows you to view and edit the actual HTML tags for any page.

1 With the HOME.HTM window still visible and active, choose Edit > HTML Source.

2 Choose Edit > HTML Source again to display the page.

Viewing the Home page in a Web browser

Now that you've completed the Home page, you can view it in the Web browser to make sure it is formatted properly. PageMill lets you display the currently active window in a specified Web browser.

1 Choose View > Switch To (Windows) or Window > Switch To (MacOS), then choose a Web browser.

If a Web browser name doesn't appear in the Switch To menu, make sure you have properly set this preference. For more information, see "Setting PageMill preferences" on page 5.

2 The Web browser starts and the Home page appears in the browser window, just as other visitors to the Web site will see it.

The title you typed earlier in the lesson appears in the browser title bar.

3 Click the HOME.HTM window in PageMill to make it active.

Now you'll end the lesson.

4 Close both the Inspector and Color Panel palettes.

5 Choose File > Close.

Review questions

1 What are three benefits of giving a Web page a name that's separate from the filename?

2 What controls the format and style of text on a Web page when it's viewed in a Web browser?

3 How do you duplicate an object on a page?

Answers

1 A Web browser uses a page title for the name it displays in its title bar, for a bookmark, and in a list of pages the user has visited, which is sometimes called a History list.

2 HTML formats specify relative sizes and formatting. Users specify fonts, sizes, and colors in the Web browser preferences.

3 You can duplicate an object in two ways:

• Select the object, hold down Ctrl (Windows) or Option (MacOS) and drag to an empty paragraph.

• Select the object, choose Edit > Copy, click an insertion point in an empty paragraph, and choose Edit > Paste.

Lesson 2

Adding Links to and From the Home Page

Links are one of the most significant differences between printed pages and Web pages. They allow immediate access to related information, and they add interactivity to documents.

In the first lesson you learned about basic text and image features available in PageMill. In this lesson you'll go on to learn about a feature just as important as text and images: links.

By clicking on links, users can follow their own paths from one block of information to the next. Instead of having one page follow another, as in a printed book, several links may be added to each page, with each link leading directly to another page containing links to even more pages. You can link pages into the most appropriate structure for the information you are conveying.

Web pages can contain links to other Web pages or to other parts of the same page. A link is a specially marked portion of a page—a single word, a sentence, or an image—that has been connected to another page. When you click a link, the Web browser takes you to the destination page for the link. In PageMill, creating a link can be as simple as dragging the icon of a page onto selected text or an image.

This lesson gets you started with links. In it, you'll learn to:

• Use both Preview mode and Edit mode

• Follow links

• Create a link by dragging and dropping page icons

• Move and edit linked text

• Change the color of linked text

• Store a linked item on the Pasteboard

Opening and exploring the Offerings page

In the first lesson you created the Home page, which included a navigation bar so that visitors to the Web site can easily move to different pages in the site. Later in this lesson, you'll link the section names in the navigation bar to different pages in the site. You'll start by exploring how a link works. One link has been created for you: it jumps from the Offerings section of the site back to the Home page.

1 Start PageMill, if necessary, then close the Untitled window.

2 Choose File > Open, locate and open the Lesson2 folder in the WEBSITE folder, then double-click the OFFERING.HTM file.

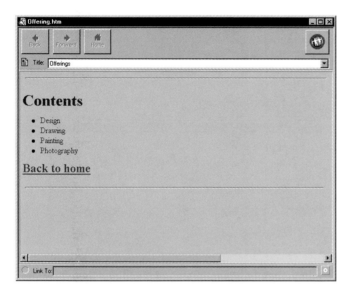

About Preview and Edit modes

An existing document opens in Preview mode, as indicated by the Globe icon (⊕) in the toolbar. In Preview mode, you can view the page and follow its links; the page looks and behaves as it would when viewed in a Web browser.

In Preview mode, PageMill also simulates the controls you will find in a Web browser, including the following:

Back and Forward buttons These buttons back up or advance one page along any sequence of pages that you've followed by clicking on links. The Forward button is active only after you have clicked the Back button.

Home button This button works a little differently than it does in Web browsers. Clicking the Home button in PageMill takes you to the first page from which you clicked a link.

History menu This menu lists the pages you have visited, in the order you visited them. To go to any page, just select it from the list.

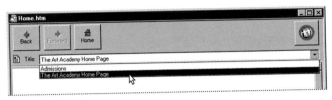

Example of a History menu

Just as you cannot change the content of the sites you visit using your Web browser—you can only view the pages and follow links— in PageMill you cannot make revisions to the current document until you switch from Preview mode to Edit mode.

In Edit mode, you are free to change almost any aspect of the page, including how it links to other destinations, but you cannot actually follow a link, as you can in Preview mode.

Switching between modes

You switch between the modes by clicking the large Globe icon on the right side of the toolbar. Typically, when creating a Web page, you'll switch back and forth between the two modes to create and test links.

1 In the OFFERING.HTM window, position the cursor over the large, underlined text "Back to Home" but don't click.

When you position the pointer over linked text or images in Preview mode, two important things happen:

• The cursor turns into a pointing hand, indicating that if you click the text you will jump to the link's destination.

• The Link To bar at the bottom of the window displays the link's destination.

2 Click the linked text "Back to Home."

The HOME.HTM page opens in Preview mode, replacing the contents of the window. In addition to testing, you'll find that clicking links makes editing easier, since you can quickly open pages. For this reason, many Web page designers like to set up their links early in the project.

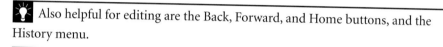 Also helpful for editing are the Back, Forward, and Home buttons, and the History menu.

Creating and editing links

A link is simply a connection between a source and destination. The source is the text or image, which, when clicked, makes PageMill (or a Web browser) display the destination—for example, another Web page. Displaying the destination is sometimes called "jumping." The destination can be another page, a downloadable file, or any Uniform Resource Locator (URL). A URL is an address to a specific file or location on the Web that is outside the local Web site.

When you create a link, you always start by identifying the source. The next step is to identify the destination. You'll now create a link from the Home page to the Offerings page.

1 Choose File > Open, locate the OFFERING.HTM file in the Lesson2 folder, and double-click.

 In Windows, you can also select the OFFERING.HTM file from the list at the bottom of the File menu.

2 Choose Window > Tile Vertically (Windows) or Window > Tile (MacOS) to view both the HOME.HTM and the OFFERING.HTM windows simultaneously.

 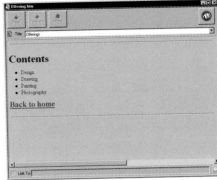

3 Click the HOME.HTM window to make it active, then click the Preview icon.

The icon changes from the Preview mode icon (⊚) to the Edit mode icon (✍), indicating that PageMill is now in Edit mode.

The tools in the toolbar now become available—remember that if you slowly move the pointer over a toolbar button or icon, text below or on the right briefly identifies each control.

4 Scroll down, if necessary, to view the navigation bar text.

5 Select the words "Academic Offerings."(Do not select the opening or closing bracket, nor the spaces between the bracket and the text.)

You are about to make the text "Academic Offerings" jump to the OFFERING.HTM page.

First, notice the small icon that looks like a page in the upper left of each PageMill window. This is the Page-link icon (📄), and you use it to represent the destination of a link. You'll simply drag the icon to the source of the link—the text or image you want to jump to another page.

6 From the OFFERING.HTM window, drag the Page-link icon from the toolbar onto the selected text in the HOME.HTM window. When the insertion point is visible in the text, release the mouse button.

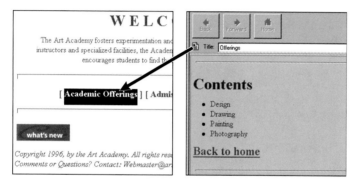

The selected text changes color and becomes underlined, indicating that it is linked. The Link To bar along the bottom of the HOME.HTM window displays the destination filename.

7 Click on the page (but not on the selected text) to deselect the text.

Changing the color of links

In PageMill and Web browsers, links are usually specified to display in a color different from regular text on the page. In addition, links that have been clicked are displayed in Web browsers in a third color, so users can remember which links they've visited. The default color for links is blue, and the default color for visited links is purple. Remember, however, that users can change the color of text, including links, to anything they want in their Web browser.

Note: PageMill does not display visited links in a different color.

Next, you'll return to the Inspector and change the color of links on the Home page.

1 Choose View > Show Inspector and View > Show Color Panel (Windows) or Window > Show Inspector and Window > Show Color Panel (MacOS).

In place of the default colors, you can create custom colors for the Color Panel palette. You'll create a custom color, then assign it to links.

2 In the Color Panel, double-click the white color. The Color dialog box appears.

3 In the dialog box, select a reddish-brown color.

4 Click OK to close the dialog box.

The color you just defined replaces the white color you double-clicked in the Color Panel.

5 Now drag the color you defined onto the Normal Links menu in the Inspector. If you inadvertently drag the color to the wrong menu, choose Edit > Undo (Windows) or Edit > Undo Link Color (MacOS), and drag the color again.

The links on the page change color.

6 Choose File > Save Page.

7 Close both the Inspector and Color Panel palettes to clear your work area.

Now you'll test a link by switching to Preview mode.

8 If necessary, click the OFFERING.HTM window to make it active, then choose File > Close, or click the close box so that only the HOME.HTM window is visible.

9 Maximize the HOME.HTM window.

10 In the HOME.HTM window, click the Edit icon to switch to Preview mode.

11 Move the pointer over the text "Academic Offerings" and click the text.

The Offerings page appears, replacing the Home page. You have succeeded in creating your first link!

By default, clicking a link in PageMill (and Web browsers) displays the new page in the same window, replacing the current contents. Sometimes, however, when testing links while editing pages, you may want to display the new page in a second window. You'll try this on the same link.

12 Click the linked text "Back to Home" in the OFFERING.HTM window. The Home page appears, replacing the Offerings page.

13 Instead of clicking the "Academic Offerings" link, hold down the mouse button on the link. (In Windows, hold down the right mouse button.) In the menu that appears, choose New Window.

The Offerings page now appears in a separate window. In Windows, the OFFERING.HTM window overlaps the HOME.HTM window.

14 Close the OFFERING.HTM window, and then maximize the HOME.HTM window, if necessary.

Moving and modifying linked text

As you'll learn in this section, you can edit a linked item freely. The main thing to remember is that if the destination is renamed or moved to a different location, the link will be broken. You'll learn how to correct a broken link in later lessons.

To edit a link, you must select its text. For most changes, it's important to select the entire set of linked characters. You can do that quickly in Edit mode by simply triple-clicking anywhere in the link. (If you triple-click in unlinked text, the entire line of text is selected.)

As you might have noticed, the large Art Academy logo at the top of the page lists Admissions as the first section, while the navigation bar lists Academic Offerings as the first section. To make the navigation bar more consistent, you'll move and edit the linked text so that it matches the order and wording of the image.

1 If necessary, click the Preview icon to switch to Edit mode.

2 In Edit mode, triple-click the text "Academic Offerings."

This selects the entire link. Note that the Link To bar displays the link destination. All the characters in the link must be selected to display the destination.

3 Drag the selected text "Academic Offerings" to the right, and when the insertion point appears directly to the left of the word "Admissions," release the mouse button.

Drag the selected the text to the right…

then release the mouse button.

Now you'll move the Admissions section to its own set of brackets.

4 Select the text "Admissions." (Do not select the space immediately after the word.)

5 Drag the selected text to the left, and when the insertion point appears in the center of the empty set of brackets at the start of the line, release the mouse button.

Drag the selected text to the left…

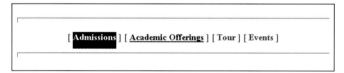

then release the mouse button.

The link is still preserved, as you'll see in a few minutes when you test it. And it will still be preserved even when you edit the text in the next step.

6 Select the word "Academic," including the space after it. (There's no need to triple-click since we want to delete this word, not the link itself.)

7 Press Delete, so the navigation bar text now says "Offerings."

[Admissions] [**Offerings**] [Tour] [Events]

Now it's time to create a new link.

Linking the Home page to the Admissions page

To link the Home page to the Admissions page, you first select the source, just as you did earlier when linking to the Offerings page, and then you'll bring the destination to the source.

1 Double-click the text "Admissions" in the navigation bar to select it.

2 Choose File > Open, then locate and double-click the file ADMISSNS.HTM in the Lesson2 folder.

3 When the ADMISSNS.HTM window appears, click the Preview icon to switch to Edit mode.

4 Choose Window > Tile Vertically (Windows) or Window > Tile (MacOS).

5 If tiling changed your view of the HOME.HTM window so that the "Admissions" text is no longer visible, scroll to bring that text into view.

6 Drag the Page-link icon from the toolbar in the ADMISSNS.HTM window onto the selected "Admissions" text in the HOME.HTM window, and release the mouse button.

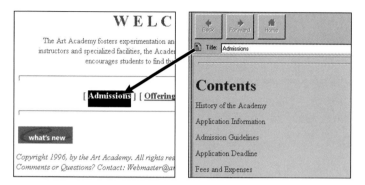

The "Admissions" text becomes underlined and changes color. Another link is established.

7 If necessary, click the ADMISSNS.HTM window to make it active, and then choose File > Close, or click the close box so that only the HOME.HTM window is visible. Maximize the HOME.HTM window, if necessary.

8 Choose File > Save Page to accept the changes to the Home page.

Now you'll test the links.

9 In the HOME.HTM window, click the Edit icon to switch to Preview mode.

10 Click the linked text "Admissions."

11 The Admissions page opens in the same window, replacing the Home page. This is the default behavior for Web browsers.

12 Click the Back button at the top of the window to return to the Home page, scroll to the link "Offerings" (if necessary), then click the link.

The Offerings page appears.

Linking images

You can also link images using the same techniques you learned with text. At this point the Art Academy Home page links to the Admissions page and to the Offerings page. And the Offerings page links back to the Home page. The link that is missing is to connect the Admissions page back to the Home page. You'll create that link now using an image rather than text.

1 In the OFFERING.HTM window, click the linked text "Back to Home" to return to the Home page.

2 In the HOME.HTM window, scroll, if necessary, to display the linked text "Admissions."

3 Position the pointer over the link, hold down the mouse button (the right mouse button in Windows), and choose New Window from the menu.

The Admissions page appears in a new window.

4 Choose Window > Tile Vertically (Windows) or Window > Tile (MacOS) to view the windows simultaneously.

5 In the ADMISSNS.HTM window, scroll, if necessary, to display the Return Home image representing the Home page.

6 Click the Preview icon to switch to Edit mode.

7 Click the "Return Home" image to select it.

8 Drag the Page-link icon from the HOME.HTM window to the selected Return Home image in the ADMISSNS.HTM window. When the tip of the pointer is inside the image, release the mouse button.

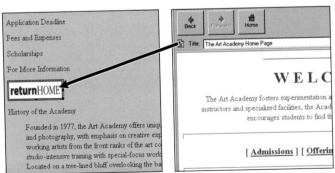

The border of the image appears in the color selected for Normal links. Now you'll test this link.

9 If necessary, click the HOME.HTM window to make it active, and then choose File > Close, or click the Close box so that only the ADMISSNS.HTM window is visible.

10 In the ADMISSNS.HTM window, click the Edit icon to return to Preview mode.

11 Choose File > Save Page.

12 Click the image you just linked.

The Home page is displayed in the window; the link is working correctly. Your next step is to replace the linked text Back to Home Page in the Offerings page with the linked image representing the Home page.

Using the Pasteboard to store and reuse items

Since you'll want most pages in the Art Academy Web site to provide access back to the Home page, you'll now store the image where it is easily accessible regardless of which page windows are open. PageMill provides a Pasteboard feature for this purpose. The Pasteboard is like the Clipboard, but more versatile—you can store different objects there at once. And, because the Pasteboard is a floating palette, you can readily see the items available to be brought onto your page.

1 In the HOME.HTM window, click the "Admissions" link to open the Admissions page.

2 Click the Preview icon to switch to Edit mode.

3 Choose View > Show Pasteboard (Windows) or Window > Show Pasteboard (MacOS).

4 Drag the "Return Home" image from the Admissions page to the Pasteboard.

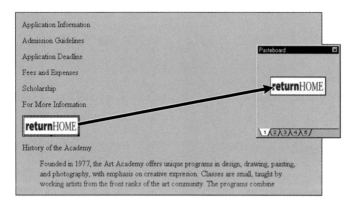

Notice that the image maintains its link on the Pasteboard, as indicated by the colored border.

5 In the ADMISSNS.HTM window, click the Edit icon to switch to Preview mode, then click the linked "Return Home" image to return to the HOME.HTM contents.

6 Click the "Offerings" link in the navigation bar.

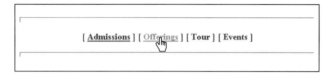

7 After the Offerings page appears, click the Preview icon to switch to Edit mode. You need to edit the page to make room for the Return Home image.

8 Find the "Back to Home" text.

9 Triple-click within the linked text (to ensure that you select the entire link), and press Delete.

10 Click an insertion point in the empty paragraph above the bottom rule.

You'll add the linked image into this paragraph.

11 To create a copy of the image, hold down Ctrl (Windows) or Option (MacOS) and drag the image from the Pasteboard onto the Offerings page. Release the mouse button when the insertion point appears in the empty paragraph you created in the previous step.

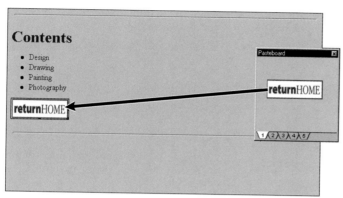

12 Close the Pasteboard.

As you learned in Lesson 1, holding down the Ctrl key (Windows) or Option key (MacOS) while dragging creates a copy of the dragged item. If you ever need to clear the Pasteboard, simply drag its contents onto a page without pressing Ctrl or Option.

13 Choose File > Save Page.

Now you're ready to test the links you've created. Note that link colors are still using the default color blue. When you changed the color of links in this lesson, you changed it for the Home page, not the Offerings page. Colors for page elements are changed only for a single page, not for every page in the Web site.

14 Click the Edit icon in the OFFERING.HTM window to switch to Preview mode.

15 Click the "Return Home" link to open the Home page.

16 When the Home page opens, click the "Admissions" link so you can test the link from the Admissions page.

17 In the Admissions page, click the "Return Home" link to return to the Home page.

You now have a full set of links interconnecting the Home page with the Admissions and Offerings pages.

18 With the Home page as the active window, choose View > Switch To (Windows) or Window > Switch To (MacOS), then select a Web browser.

The Home page opens in the Web browser window.

19 Click the "Admissions" link.

20 After the Admissions page opens, click the Back button at the top of the browser window to return to the Home page. Notice that the Admissions text is now displayed in a different color. This is the color you chose for visited links.

Lesson 2 is complete.

21 Quit the Web browser, and in PageMill, choose Window > Close All.

Review questions

1 How is viewing a page in the PageMill Preview mode like viewing a page in a Web browser?

2 What is the sequence of steps for creating a link from one PageMill page to another?

3 How do you select linked text so that you can edit it?

4 When you want to use a copy of an element that is stored on the PageMill Pasteboard, what do you do?

Answers

1 In the PageMill Preview mode, you can follow the links and navigate through the pages using the Back and Forward buttons. You can also view pages you have visited using the History menu.

2 First, select the source of the link (an image or text), then drag the Page-link icon from a different window (the link destination) onto the source.

3 In Edit mode, triple-click anywhere in the link to select the entire set of linked characters. If the linked text is within a line of text, be sure the cursor is over the linked text when you triple-click or you will select the entire line instead.

4 Hold down Ctrl (Windows) or Option (MacOS) and drag the element from the Pasteboard onto the page.

Lesson 3

Enhancing a Web Page

In this lesson, you'll enhance sections you've already created by accomplishing the same tasks in new ways.

In Lesson 1, you learned the basics of working with text and images in PageMill and then moved onto basic linking tasks in Lesson 2. In this lesson, you'll return to the text and image features, but this time explore them in more depth as you enhance the Admissions page. Specifically, you'll learn to:

- Use the Inspector to make text changes
- Apply the HTML format for bullet lists
- Use HTML heading levels to create headings and subheadings
- Align figures in a table with a monospaced text style
- Add numbers automatically to a sequential list
- Make an image transparent
- Create an interlaced GIF image
- Apply a border around an image
- Add a background image to a page

Formatting the Admissions Page

Now you'll take a more careful look at the formatting options available for text and images in an HTML document. Earlier you used the Format menu to control the look of paragraphs on the home page. Here you'll use the Inspector to apply the paragraph formats, and to apply type styles—formatting options which change a range of characters within a paragraph.

1 Start PageMill, if necessary, then close the Untitled window.

2 Choose File > Open, then locate and open the Lesson3 folder in the WEBSITE folder, and double-click the ADMISSNS.HTM file.

3 Click the Preview icon to switch to Edit mode.

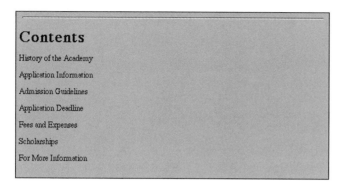

Applying list formats

You'll start with the lines below the Contents heading. The lines form a list, but it's not very appealing visually. PageMill provides several HTML list formats for handling this kind of information.

1 Select the entire list, from "History of the Academy" down to the last line, "For More Information."

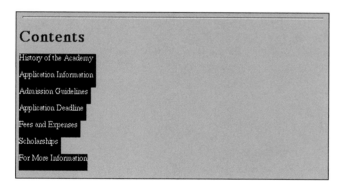

In Lesson 1, you used the Format menu in the menu bar to apply text formats. You can also use the Format menu in the toolbar to apply the same formats.

2 In the toolbar, choose Bullet List from the format menu.

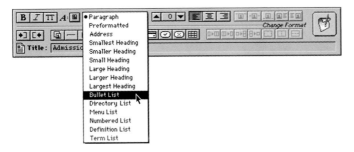

The bullets and the indent setting are applied automatically to the paragraphs.

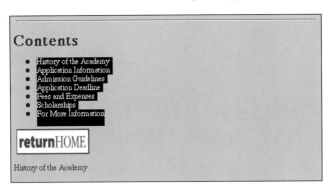

In the paragraphs you have just selected, the bullet items between "Application Information" and "For More Information" are actually subsections, and need to be indented under the "Application Information" bullet item.

3 Select the bullet items "Admissions Guidelines," "Application Deadline," "Fees and Expenses," and "Scholarships."

4 Click the Indent Right button (•⊐) in the toolbar.

The items appear with a different bullet to indicate another level of the hierarchy.

The bullet list is a commonly used format. You'll explore some of the other list formats a little later in this lesson.

Using heading levels to define subsections

The paragraphs you just formatted with the bullet list act as a small table of contents for the page. Now you'll create some of the subsections these paragraphs refer to. (In the next Lesson, you'll complete the process by linking the bulleted paragraphs at the top of the page to the subsections themselves. That way a visitor to the Web site can go directly to the information of interest, without having to scroll.)

1 If necessary, scroll to view the text "History of the Academy," which is the heading for the first subsection of the page. The text is flush left, and is not indented to the right as is most of the text below it.

2 Click an insertion point to the left of the word "History."

3 In the toolbar, choose Larger Heading from the Format menu. (The Largest Heading is typically reserved for the title of the document.)

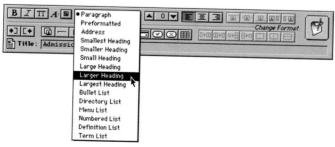

As you format these headings, you'll also give them a horizontal rule.

4 Press Enter or Return to create a paragraph for the rule.

5 Click an insertion point in the empty paragraph, and click the Insert Horizontal Rule button (—) in the toolbar.

6 Click the rule, drag the handle centered on the bottom of the rule down about one-quarter of an inch, and release the mouse button. If you inadvertently drag the entire rule, choose Edit > Undo (Windows) or Edit > Undo Drag (MacOS) and repeat this step.

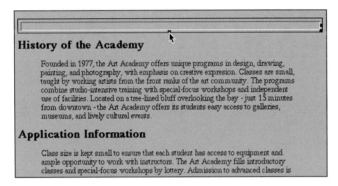

Now you'll duplicate this rule so you can use it on another section of the page.

7 Scroll down to view the next major section, Application Information, and click an insertion point just before the word "Application."

8 Press Enter or Return to create an empty paragraph for the rule.

9 Hold down Ctrl (Windows) or Option (MacOS), select the rule you created in an earlier step, and drag it into the empty paragraph.

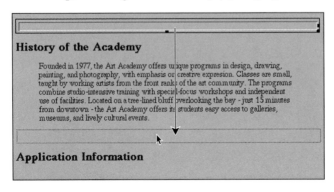

Now you'll line up the two headings with the paragraphs by indenting them. Note that HTML uses preset tabs for indenting; you can't change the spacing between the tabs.

10 Click an insertion point just before the "H" in the text "History of the Academy."

11 Click the Indent Right button (▸⌐) in the toolbar.

12 Repeat steps 10 and 11 with the Application Information heading, then choose File > Save Page.

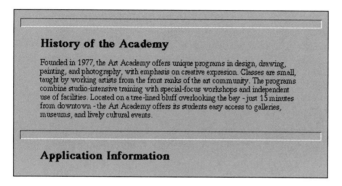

Applying a monospaced font

Further down the page is a section called Fees and Expenses. The text includes a set of dollar figures; the figures should be aligned. You can apply the Teletype style to do this. Teletype style instructs a Web browser to display a range of characters in a monospaced font—that is, a typeface in which the space between letters and the width of characters do not vary, similar to those on a typewriter. The result is that the numbers will align correctly.

1 Scroll down to bring the dollar figures into view, if necessary.

2 Drag to select the text starting with "Tuition (2 classes)...$1,550," and ending with "Total Fee...$2,400."

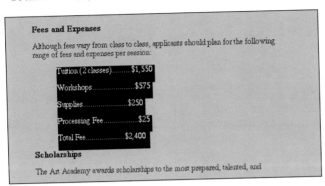

3 In the toolbar, click the Teletype button (TT). The numbers align appropriately.

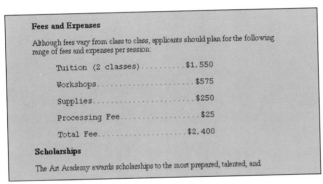

Because Teletype is a style applied to one or more characters (unlike a Format, which applies to one or more paragraphs), any heading level or list format in your document can include monospaced characters within it.

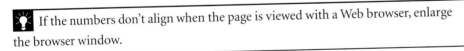 If the numbers don't align when the page is viewed with a Web browser, enlarge the browser window.

Applying a numbered list

You'll finish text formatting by applying list formats.

The Scholarship section includes a step-by-step procedure that would be easier to use if each step had a number. You can add numbers with the Numbered List format. Although you won't see the actual numbers in PageMill when you apply the format, you will see the numbers in a Web browser. You can freely add or remove paragraphs in a numbered list right up until the time you publish your Web site. Because the Web browser calculates the number of paragraphs as it opens the document, the numbering will always be accurate.

1 Scroll down the page to bring the bold heading "To apply for a scholarship" into view, along with the four lines following the heading.

2 Select the four lines following the heading.

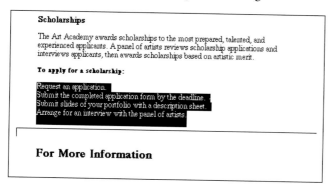

3 Choose Numbered List from the Format menu in the toolbar.

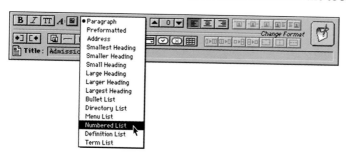

4 The list appears with number signs as placeholders for the actual figures to be inserted by the Web browser.

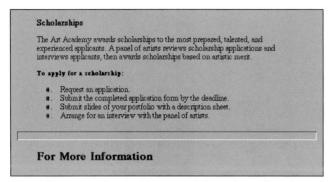

The # signs are replaced with sequential numbers when the page is viewed in a Web browser.

Assigning color to selected text

In Lesson 1, you learned how to change the background color and the color of all the text on a page. You can also specify color for selected text. You'll change the color of the first paragraph in the Admissions page.

1 Scroll to the top of the ADMISSNS.HTM window.

2 Select the heading "History of the Academy," located just beneath the second rule, not in the bullet list.

3 If the Color Panel is not visible, choose View > Show Color Panel (Windows) or Window > Show Color Panel (MacOS).

4 Select the light brown color from the Color Panel and drag the circle on to the top of the selected paragraph.

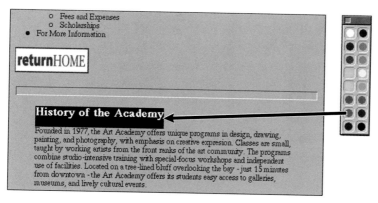

5 Click outside the paragraph to deselect it.

The heading History of the Academy now appears in the new color.

6 Choose File > Save Page.

Replacing text and checking spelling

PageMill lets you easily check spelling and find and replace text. To see how these features work, you'll begin by replacing the application deadline date shown on the Admissions page.

1 If necessary, click the Preview icon to switch to Edit mode, then choose Search > Find.

2 In the Find dialog box, make sure Page Content is selected in the top menu.

3 In the Scope menu at the bottom of the dialog box, choose Page.

4 Make sure the Wrap option is selected.

The Wrap option ensures that the entire page is searched, even if the cursor is not at the very top.

5 Deselect the Deep option.

You don't need the Deep option, which tells PageMill to search any embedded tables or form elements.

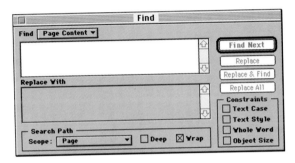

Now you'll replace the application deadline of July 26 with July 31.

6 Click an insertion point in the Find box and type **July 26**. Then press Tab.

7 Type **July 31** in the Replace With box, then click Find Next.

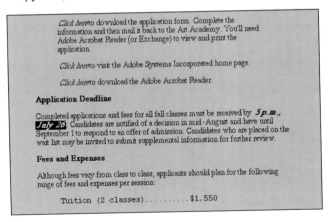

PageMill finds and highlights "July 26."

8 Click Replace to insert the new date, then close the Find dialog box.

Now you'll check for spelling errors. It's often easier to start spelling checks at the beginning of a page, so you know you've covered the whole page without repeating sections.

9 Scroll to the top of the page and click just before the first paragraph "History of the Academy." PageMill will start checking at the insertion point.

10 Choose Search > Check Spelling.

11 At the bottom of the Spell Check dialog box, deselect the Wrap option. Since you're starting at the top of the page, you don't need the search to wrap around to the beginning again.

PageMill finds that the word "expression" has been misspelled with only one "s."

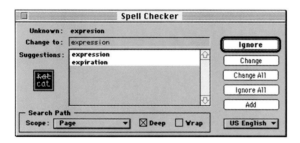

12 To correct the spelling, select the correct word and click Change.

13 If PageMill does not recognize a word, it marks it as misspelled. The next misspelled word it finds is "35mm." Since you know this is correct, click Ignore.

14 Click Ignore for each of the next three words PageMill marks as misspelled. These words form the e-mail address and are certainly not found in any dictionary.

When you reach the end of the page, the Spell Checker dialog box reports that there are no more unknown words.

15 Close the Spell Checker dialog box.

Wrapping text around an image

To create more appealing page designs, especially those with a lot of text, you can insert one or more images on the left or right side of a paragraph so that text flows around them.

You'll insert a couple of images into a paragraph on the Admissions page.

1 In the ADMISSNS.HTM window, scroll up to the section History of the Academy and select the "F" in the word "Founded" at the beginning of the paragraph.

2 Click the Place Object button (⌦) in the toolbar, locate and open the Images folder in the Lesson3 folder, then double-click the DROPCAP.GIF file.

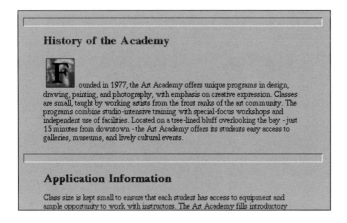

By default the image is placed to the left of the paragraph, at the baseline of the first line. Instead, you'll align the text with the top of the image.

3 Select the drop cap image you just inserted.

Page Mill provides buttons at the top of the window for aligning an image with text. By default, the Bottom Align Object button is selected.

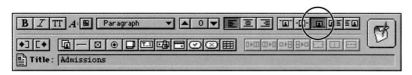

4 Click the Left Align Object button (⊞≣) in the toolbar.

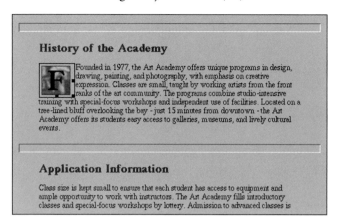

The text now starts at the top of the image and wraps around it for a more appealing paragraph.

Now you'll add an image on the right side of the paragraph. To place it in an appealing position, you'll insert it toward the end of the first sentence.

5 Click an insertion point at the end of the first sentence in the same paragraph, just before the word "expression."

6 Once again, click the Place Object button in the toolbar, then double-click the DUOBLDG.GIF file in the Images folder.

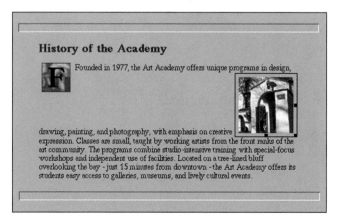

7 Select the image you just inserted.

8 This time, click the Right Align Object button (≡▣) in the toolbar.

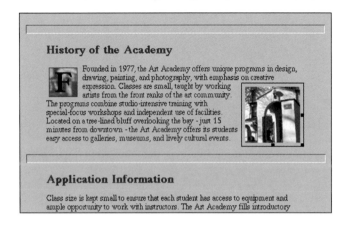

The image is now placed on the right side of the paragraph, with text flowing around it.

9 Choose File > Save Page.

Now you'll apply some more image features to enhance the page even further.

Enhancing the Admissions page with images

In the following procedures, you'll learn a little more about effects you can apply to images and new ways of performing some of the tasks you learned in Lesson 1. You'll start by inserting a banner image to span the top of the Admissions page. You'll also enhance the Contents heading by replacing it with an image.

1 Scroll to the top of the page and click an insertion point in the upper left corner of the page, just before the narrow rule above the Contents heading.

Now you'll add an image in the space above the first rule on the page.

2 Click the Place Object button, then double-click the ADMSLOGO.GIF file in the Images folder.

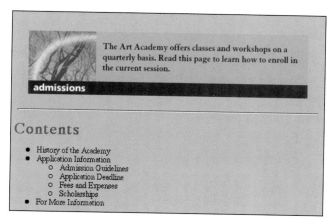

Next you'll replace the Contents heading with an image so you can apply effects to the image in the next section of this lesson.

3 Select the text "Contents" beneath the rule at the top of the page.

4 Click the Place Object button, then double-click the CONTENTS.GIF file in the Images folder.

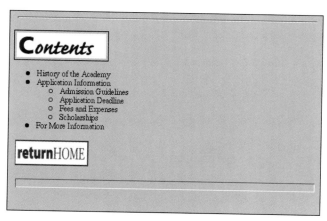

Making an image transparent

In Lesson 1 you left the image that you placed just as it was created, only slightly resized. But PageMill lets you modify images to take advantage of Web browser capabilities. In the next step, you'll make a part of the opaque Contents image transparent. Transparency lets you set a color in an image to be transparent by turning all pixels in the selected color transparent. Transparency also lets you use the background color of the page in your images.

Note: *Only GIF files support transparency; JPEG files do not.*

1 In the ADMISSNS.HTM window, hold down Ctrl (Windows) or Command (MacOS), then double-click the "Contents" image you just added to the Admissions page.

The image appears in an image-editing window. The window includes several tools, most of which concern image links. You'll explore the image link tools in a later lesson.

2 Click the Make Transparent tool (✎) in the toolbar along the left edge of the image-editing window.

3 Click on a part of the image that is white.

Notice that the color white is no longer opaque in the image-editing window. All the pixels in the image that contain the color you clicked with the Make Transparent tool turned transparent; if you click a transparent area, the color is restored.

Click on the background color...   *to make it transparent.*

Once you save this change, you'll see its effect in the ADMISSNS.HTM window. Note that when you've made changes in the image-editing window, you save the changes by choosing File > Save Image. In addition, the File > Close command applies to the image you are working on, not to the page.

4 Choose File > Save Image.

Notice how the background of the page shows through the areas of the image that you made transparent.

5 Close the image-editing window.

Adding a border

Here you'll learn one technique you can use within PageMill to modify an image as it appears only on a particular page, rather than creating effects that alter the image's appearance throughout the Web site. You'll now add a border surrounding the selected image.

1 Scroll down to the History of the Academy section in the ADMISSNS.HTM window.

2 Select the image on the right side of the paragraph.

3 Choose View > Show Inspector (Windows) or Window > Show Inspector (MacOS), if the Inspector is not visible. The Object tab (■) should be selected.

Click in the Border text box at the bottom of the palette, and type 2. This defines a border two pixels wide.

4 Press Tab, or press Enter or Return to apply the border.

 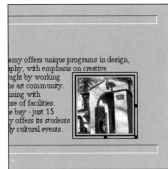

Select the image…   *then apply a border.*

The border appears. The color of text on the page determines the color of any image border on the page. If you copy the image to another window, it will retain the border width, but take on the color applied to text on the page.

Note: *If you want to remove a border from a linked image, you can set the border to 0 pixels in the Inspector.*

Adding a tiled background to the page

In Lesson 1 you learned how to replace the gray page background with a color. PageMill also lets you use an image as a background for a page. The image is tiled (repeated) as often as needed to fill the page. Background images can significantly enhance the appearance of Web-based publications. You'll add a background image using the Inspector.

1 If necessary, resize or move the ADMISSNS.HTM window and the Inspector so that the Images folder in the Lesson3 folder is visible in Explorer (Windows) or Finder (MacOS).

2 Click the Page tab (▢) in the Inspector.

3 In the Images folder, locate the ADMSTILE.GIF image.

4 Drag the image to the background box in the Inspector, and drop the image into place.

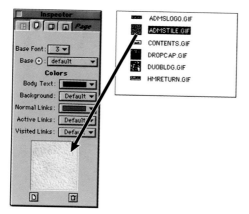

The image is arranged horizontally left to right and then top to bottom to fill the page completely.

If you inadvertently selected the wrong image from the Images folder, click Clear (Windows) or the Trash button (🗑) (MacOS) in the Inspector to delete that background. Then repeat the procedure with the correct image.

Creating an interlaced image

If your image is a GIF file, you can save it so it downloads in layers, producing a venetian-blind effect, rather than downloading each line in sequence. At first, the image looks coarse; as each layer is added, it becomes sharper until it reaches its full resolution. Interlaced images prevent the reader from seeing an empty page while a large image downloads. Web browsers that do not support interlacing can still display interlaced GIFs, but without the interlacing effect.

Note: JPEG files do not support interlacing.

1 Scroll up to the banner image you added at the top of the ADMISSNS.HTM window.

2 Hold down Ctrl (Windows) or Command (MacOS) and double-click the image.

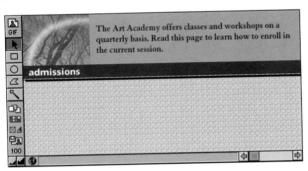

3 In the image-editing window for the ADMSLOGO.GIF, click the Make Interlaced button (⌨).

In Windows, the icon appears selected to indicate interlacing. In MacOS, the icon changes to a striped appearance. The image itself does not change.

4 With the ADMSLOGO.GIF window active, choose File > Save Image, and then close the image-editing window.

The Admissions page is complete!

5 Choose File > Save Page to accept the changes you've made to this page.

You cannot preview the interlaced effect in PageMill. To see the interlaced effect, you must load the page in a Web browser that supports interlaced GIF files. If you have installed a Web browser, you can see the interlaced effect now.

6 With the Admissions page still open, choose View > Switch To (Windows) or Window > Switch To (MacOS), then select a Web browser.

As the page opens, you should see the image displayed in layers until it is completely visible. The effect is not as noticeable when downloading files stored locally, but is intended for longer downloading times across busy networks.

7 Quit the Web browser, then close the ADMISSNS.HTM window.

Review questions

1 How do you change a list of items to a bullet list?

2 If you want a heading to be bigger and a different color than the text below it, what do you do?

3 How do you wrap text around a drop cap?

4 The banner image you just inserted has a white background. How do you make the image background match the page background?

5 What determines the color of any image border on the page?

Answers

1 Select the entire list of items, then choose Bullet List from the Format menu in either the menu bar or the toolbar.

2 To change the size of the heading, click an insertion point anywhere in the heading and choose a heading option (such as Larger Heading) from the Format menu in either the menu bar or the toolbar. To change the color of the heading, select the heading, open the Color Panel, and drag a color to the heading.

3 Select the drop cap, then click the Left Align Object button in the toolbar.

4 Hold down Ctrl (Windows) or Command (MacOS), then double-click on the banner image to display the image-editing window. Click the Make Transparent tool in the toolbar along the left side of the window, and click anywhere on the white background.

5 The color of text on the page determines the color of the image border.

Lesson 4:

Using Anchors

So far, the links in the Art Academy Web site jump from one page to another, always opening the specified page at the top. By using markers called anchors, however, you can link to any location on a page.

On the Web, a page can be virtually any length. It's often desirable or necessary to link to a specific location within a particular page. This lesson will focus on linking to subsections within the Admissions page. Specifically, you'll learn to:

• Show and hide anchors

• Add anchors to a page

• Link to anchors

Understanding anchors

PageMill uses markers called *anchors* that let you link to specified points anywhere on a Web page. Anchors expand the options you have for linking, so that you can make information more accessible and easy to find.

As an example, you'll look at a page that puts anchors to good use—the Events page.

1 Start PageMill, if necessary, then close the Untitled window.

2 Choose File > Open, open and locate the Lesson4 folder in the WEBSITE folder, then double-click the EVENTS.HTM file.

3 Use the scroll bar to move down the page, or press the Page Down key on your keyboard.

The page discusses three events: Exhibition Schedule, Lecture Series, and an Open House. Each section ends with linked text that returns you to the top of the page.

Exhibition Schedule

November 4 to November 30, 1997

The Art Academy will present a selection of student works from the current session in the campus Gallery. The purpose of the exhibition is to introduce new visual arts talent to the community. A reception celebrating these works will be the current session in the campus Gallery. The purpose held at the Gallery on Monday, November 4, from 6 to 8 p.m.

Click here to download the invitation. You'll need Adobe Acrobat Reader (or Exchange) to view the document.

Click here to visit the Adobe Systems Incorporated home page.

Click here to download the Adobe Acrobat Reader.

return to top

4 Once you've looked at these sections, scroll to the top of the page.

Now you'll move around the page by using links.

5 Click the "Lecture Series" link.

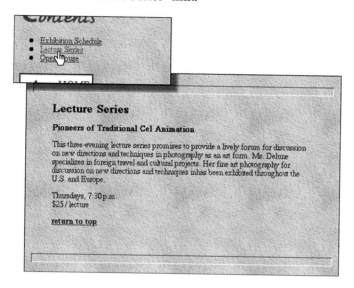

The page moves to the Lecture Series section.

6 At the end of the Lecture Series section, click the "return to top" link.

The page moves back to the top.

Moving around a page using anchors is often easier than scrolling, especially with large pages. Links from other pages, too, can take you to an anchor anywhere on the destination page. Anchors offer more navigational choices to the viewer.

Viewing the anchors

Now you'll leave Preview mode so you can view the anchors that make it possible to link within a page. Anchors are not visible in Preview mode, since it wouldn't make sense to see them in a Web browser—anchors work behind the scene.

1 If the top of the page is not visible, scroll there now.

2 Click the Preview icon to switch to Edit mode.

Look at the very top of the page. There you will see a small icon in the shape of a ship's anchor (⚓). This icon represents an anchor that has been placed on the page. The anchor at the top is the one that took you back to the top of the page when you clicked the "return to top" link.

3 If the Inspector and Color Panel palettes are in the way, close them now. Then scroll down the page and note that just above each rule there is an anchor. Each of these anchors is a link to the section below it.

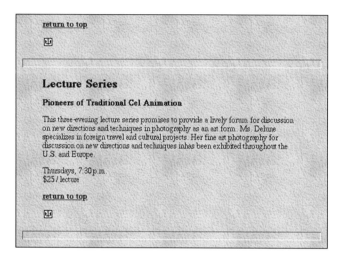

4 Close the EVENTS.HTM window.

Adding anchors to complete the Admissions page

Now you'll go back to the Admissions page and add some anchors to make it easier to move quickly to different sections on the page.

You'll make the bullet list at the top of the page into a series of links that take you to the appropriate sections below.

1 Choose File > Open, then locate and double-click the ADMISSNS.HTM file in the Lesson4 folder.

2 Click the Preview icon to switch to Edit mode.

3 Find the rule above the History of the Academy section.

4 Click an insertion point at the beginning of the rule.

5 Choose Edit > Insert Invisible > Anchor.

An anchor appears above the rule.

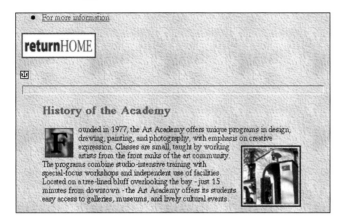

6 At the top of the page, select the bulleted text "History of the Academy" underneath the Contents heading.

As you learned in Lesson 2, you link two documents by first selecting the source text or image, and then dragging the Page-link icon from a different window (the link destination) onto the source. Linking with anchors is similar: Now that you've selected the source text or image, you'll drag the anchor onto the selection.

7 Drag the anchor that you just inserted onto the selected text.

The bulleted item displays as a link. The anchor itself has not moved.

Now you can test the link.

1 Click the Edit icon to switch to Preview mode.

2 Click the linked bulleted item "History of the Academy."

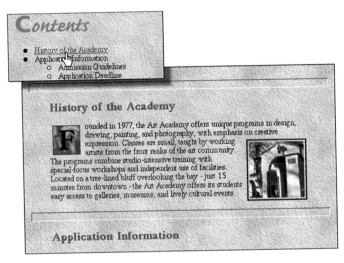

The window automatically scrolls to the anchor. Note that you placed the anchor just above the rule, so that the rule is displayed when you click the link. The rule helps define the section.

If you later decide that you want to move the anchor for this section to a different position, you can drag the anchor to the new position. But you don't need to re-link the anchor. The link will follow the anchor, wherever it is placed on the page.

3 Choose File > Save Page.

Linking the History of the Academy section back to the top of the page

In this lesson, you'll not only insert anchors and link to them, but you'll link each section in turn back to the top of the page. In most cases, when you create a link to a destination, you should also create a link back to the source.

1 Click the Preview icon to switch to Edit mode.

2 Scroll to the For More Information section at the bottom of the page.

3 This section has been completed for you. The text "return to top" at the end of the section links to an anchor at the top of the page. You'll now copy this text into another part of the page.

4 Select the text "return to top" and choose Edit > Copy.

5 Scroll up to the end of the History of the Academy section (it's marked by a horizontal rule).

6 Click an insertion point at the end of the paragraph (to the right of the words "cultural events") and press Enter or Return.

7 Choose Edit > Paste.

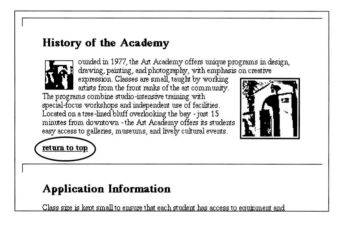

Since you'll need this text and its link for the other subsection on the page, you'll now store it on the Pasteboard.

8 Select the linked text "return to top."

9 Choose View > Show Pasteboard (Windows) or Window > Show Pasteboard (MacOS). Click the page 2 tab at the bottom of the Pasteboard (Windows) or the page turn icon (MacOS) to display a fresh page in the Pasteboard.

10 Drag the text onto the Pasteboard. The text and its link are now stored for later use.

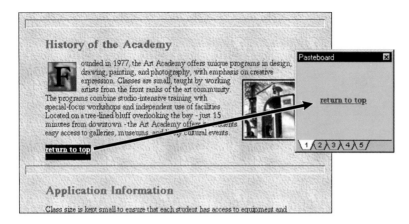

Adding and naming an anchor

Now you'll link an anchor in a slightly different way for the Application Information section.

1 Scroll to the top of the page.

2 Click an insertion point before the words "Application Information" in the bullet list.

3 Choose Edit > Insert Invisible > Anchor.

If you're including several links to anchors on the same page, keeping track of anchors becomes more important. You want to make sure that each link is jumping to the correct anchor.

To help you keep track of links and anchors, you can give each anchor a descriptive name. The anchor name is displayed in the Link To bar when you select its link.

4 Click to select the anchor you just inserted.

5 If necessary, choose View > Show Inspector (Windows) or Window > Show Inspector (MacOS).

The Inspector displays the Anchor Name text box.

PageMill automatically gives each anchor a name—the word "anchor" followed by a number. You can type a more descriptive name using the Inspector, or you can copy and paste text. You'll copy and paste the name of the link.

Note: An anchor name must use alphanumeric characters only. Special characters, such as the pound sign, may cause the anchor not to link correctly in PageMill or a Web browser.

6 Drag to select the bulleted text "Application Information," but do not include the anchor in the selection.

7 Choose Edit > Copy.

8 Select the anchor again. Then, in the Inspector, drag to select the default anchor name in the Anchor Name text box.

9 Choose Edit > Paste to overwrite the default name. Press Enter or Return to accept the change.

You've named the anchor. Now you'll establish the link.

10 Once again, drag to select the bulleted text "Application Information," but do not include the anchor in the selection.

11 Drag the anchor onto the selected text, then click in a blank area to deselect the text.

The text becomes underlined to indicate that it is linked to the anchor. Notice, too, that the link destination—the anchor name—is displayed in the Link To bar.

Next you'll position the anchor beside the correct destination—the Application Information heading lower on the page.

When you added the link to the History of the Academy section, the source of the link and the link destination were so close to each other that dragging the anchor did not require scrolling the window. With Application Information though, there's more distance between the source and the destination of the link, and scrolling the window while dragging the anchor can be cumbersome. To avoid dragging while scrolling, you can cut and paste to move the anchor.

12 Click to select the anchor at the start of the bulleted text "Application Information," and choose Edit > Cut.

13 Scroll or press the Page Down key on your keyboard so that the "Application Information" appears along with the rule above it.

14 Click an insertion point at the left end of the rule above the heading "Application Information."

15 Choose Edit > Paste to paste the anchor.

You have simply moved the link destination—the anchor—into the correct position.

Now you'll test the link again.

16 Click the Edit icon to switch to Preview mode.

17 Scroll upward, if necessary, and click the text "return to top."

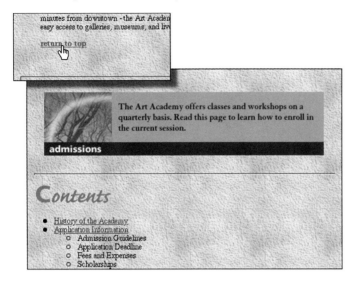

The window scrolls to the top of the page.

18 Click the linked bulleted item "Application Information."

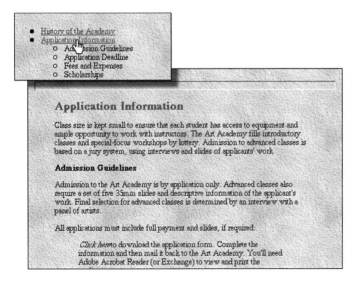

The paragraph in which the anchor had been positioned becomes the topmost paragraph in the window.

19 Click the Preview icon to return to Edit mode.

Completing the links for the Application Information section

Now you'll link this section back to the top of the page. The steps do not differ substantially from those you used to complete the links for the History of the Academy section.

1 Scroll down through the Application Information section (not the bulleted text) to bring the Scholarships section into view.

2 Click an insertion point at the end of the last sentence in the numbered list (after "...panel of artists.") and press Enter or Return.

3 Ctrl-drag (Windows) or Option-drag (MacOS) the linked text from the Pasteboard into the empty paragraph you just created. This drags a copy of the text.

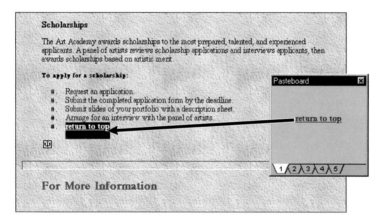

The text appears. The Link To bar indicates that the link is intact.

Now you'll adjust the text format.

4 With the text still selected, choose Paragraph from the Format menu in the toolbar.

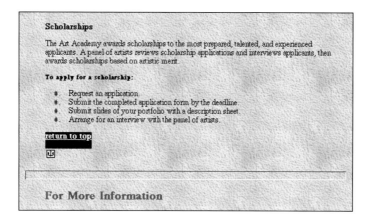

You've completed the links for the bullet list. The last item in the list, For More Information, has been completed for you.

5 Close the Pasteboard, then choose File > Save Page.

Linking from the Campus page to an anchor on the Admissions page

So far you've created anchors to direct visitors to different sections of the same page. But you'll sometimes want to link from one page to a particular section of another page. You'll learn to do that now by linking from the top of the Campus page to the last section of the Admissions page.

1 With the ADMISSNS.HTM window still open, choose File > Open.

2 In the Lesson4 folder, double-click the CAMPUS.HTM file.

3 Choose Window > Tile Vertically (Windows) or Window > Tile (MacOS) to display both the source and the destination page.

4 In the ADMISSNS.HTM window, click the Edit icon to switch to Preview mode so you can test the link, then click the link "For More Information" in the bullet list.

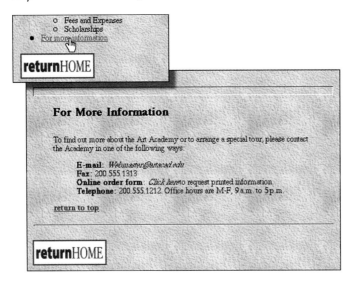

5 Click the Preview icon to switch back to Edit mode, then select the anchor above the section "For More Information."

6 Click the CAMPUS.HTM window to make it active, then click the Preview icon to switch to Edit mode.

7 In the last sentence of the paragraph at the top of the CAMPUS.HTM window, select the words "contact us." That's the source of the link you are about to create.

8 In the ADMISSNS.HTM window, drag the anchor you just selected onto the selected text in the CAMPUS.HTM window.

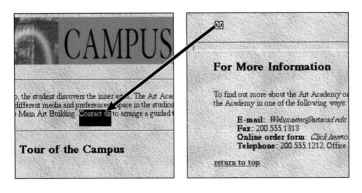

Notice what's displayed in the Link To bar at the bottom of the CAMPUS.HTM window—the name of the page followed by the anchor name.

9 With the ADMISSNS.HTM window active, choose File > Close.

10 With the CAMPUS.HTM window active, choose File > Save Page.

11 Click the Edit icon to return to Preview mode.

12 Click the linked text "Contact us."

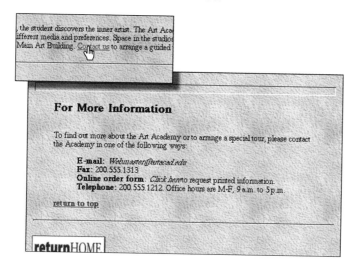

The For More Information section on the Admissions page appears.

13 Choose Window > Close. You can also close the Pasteboard and the Inspector.

Review questions

1 How do anchors increase options for linking on a Web page?

2 What is the first step in creating a link from one section of a Web page to another?

3 What PageMill tool do you use to change the default name of an anchor?

Answers

1 With anchors, you can link to specific points anywhere on a Web page. These points can be from one section to another section on the same page, or from one section on a page to another section on a different Web page.

2 You insert an anchor where the destination section is located. (The anchor is like the Page-link icon in a PageMill window.) From here, the steps are similar to linking two documents. That is, you next select the source text or image, then you drag the anchor onto the selection.

3 Once you select the anchor, you can use the Inspector to change the name in the Anchor Name text box.

Lesson 5

Creating Tables

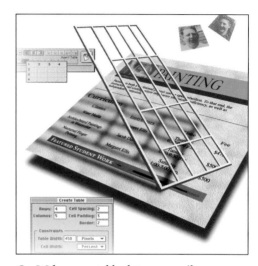

On Web pages, tables let users easily scan

information online; links inside a table can

then guide users to more detailed information

about a listed topic or summary.

Sometimes you'll need to put information in a table. On a Web page, you can place anything you like in a table: text, images, and even links. In this lesson, you'll create a table to organize information about classes and instructors. Specifically, you'll learn to:

• Create a table

• Include text, images, and links in a table cell

• Adjust table elements

• Align text and images using a table

Using tables

On a Web page, tables are best used for organizing small but related "chunks" of information into a grid that users can quickly scan. Because you often want to minimize scrolling in a Web page, information in lists can sometimes be better presented in a table. First you'll look at a page in the Art Academy site that shows an example of this.

1 Start PageMill, if necessary, then close the Untitled window.

2 Choose File > Open, locate and open the Lesson5 folder in the WEBSITE folder, then double-click the PAINTING.HTM file.

First take a look at this page to see where a table can fit. Scroll down and look at the information. You'll see that under the Painting heading is a list of classes and instructors; there are links here that jump to the bottom of the page, where you'll find more information about the classes and instructors. These links use anchors, which you learned about in Lesson 4.

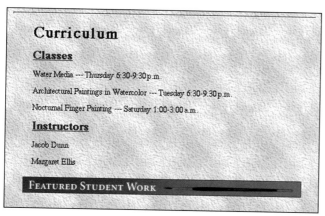

To make the information easier to scan, you'll place the class name, instructor, time, and cost in a table, which will contain links to other sections on the page. You'll place the table at the top of the page, where scanning information about classes makes the most sense.

Creating a table

Before you create a table, you need to figure out how many rows and columns you'll need. The table for class information needs four columns: Classes, Instructor, Time, and Fee.

For rows, you'll also need four: one for each of the three classes, and one for the table headings. So that gives you a table with four columns and four rows. You'll insert it just beneath the rule, above the Curriculum heading.

1 Click the Preview icon to switch to Edit mode.

2 Scroll to the top of the page in the PAINTING.HTM window, click an insertion point just to the right of the rule, then press Enter or Return. This will put a little space between the paragraph and the table.

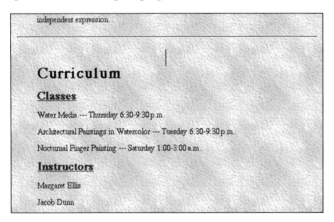

3 In the toolbar, hold the mouse down on the Insert Table button (⊞), then drag the mouse down and to the right on a diagonal to create a table that's four columns wide and four rows tall. Release the mouse button.

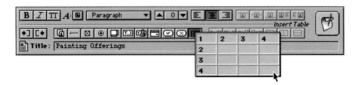

A 4x4 table appears just underneath the first paragraph. (If you inadvertently released the mouse button before getting the correct table size, just choose Edit > Undo (Windows) or Edit > Undo Insert Table (MacOS), then repeat step 3.)

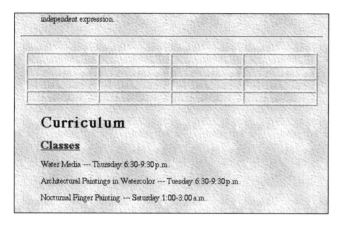

The table consists of individual cells—the rectangular areas that can contain text, images, or links. The cells are empty, but you'll add information to them in the next section.

Adding information to a table

You can add information to a table by typing text, cutting and pasting elements, or by dragging and dropping elements. You can also style text in a table just as you would style it elsewhere.

You'll add headings and class information to the table.

1 Scroll down to the Curriculum heading, so that both the table and the list of classes and instructors are visible.

2 Double-click the "Classes" link to select it, then drag the link into the upper left cell.

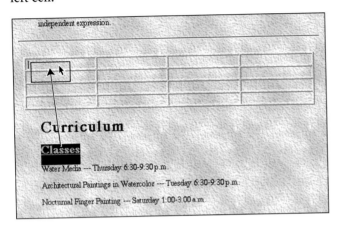

A thick textured border now surrounds the table, indicating that you are editing inside the table.

3 With the "Classes" link still selected inside the cell, choose Large Heading from the Format menu in the toolbar.

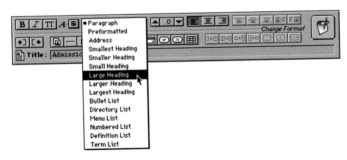

4 Next, go back to the text and double-click the "Instructors" link to select it, then drag the link into the table cell just to the right of the cell containing the "Classes" link.

5 Once again, with the linked text still selected inside the cell, choose Large Heading from the Format menu in the toolbar.

Now you'll add two more headings by typing text directly in a table cell.

6 Press Tab to advance to the cell to the right of the Instructors link and type **Time**. Then choose Large Heading from the Format menu in the toolbar.

7 Press Tab to advance to the last cell in the top row, type **Fee**, and style it as Large Heading, as you did with the other headings.

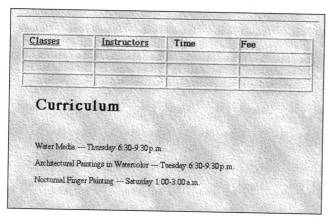

Now that you've added the table headings, you'll add information to other table cells.

8 From the first of the remaining list items, select the words "Water Media," then drag them into the cell beneath "Classes."

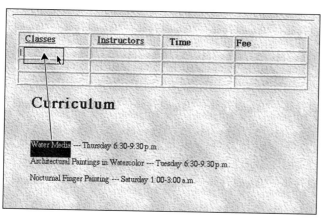

9 Now select the time for the Water Media class —Thursday 6:30-9:30 p.m.— and drag it to the cell directly beneath the "Time" heading.

The text wraps to a second line. If there is an extra space in front of the word "Thursday," just ignore it. You will center-align all the cell contents in a later procedure.

10 Repeat steps 8 and 9 for the "Architectural Paintings in Watercolor" and "Nocturnal Finger Painting" classes, placing the classes and times into the appropriate cells.

Before you add the instructors' names, you'll clean up the page a little.

11 Delete the "Curriculum" heading, the dashed lines, and the space left by the elements you moved into the table.

Your page should look like this:

Classes	Instructors	Time	Fee
Water Media		Thursday 6:30-9:30 p.m.	
Architectural Paintings in Watercolor		Tuesday 6:30-9:30 p.m.	
Nocturnal Finger Painting		Saturday 1:00-3:00 a.m.	

Margaret Ellis

Jacob Dunn

Now you'll add the instructors' names.

12 In the list, select the first instructor's name "Margaret Ellis," and drag it into the first cell under the "Instructors" heading.

13 With "Margaret Ellis" still selected in the table cell, choose Edit > Copy.

14 Click an insertion point in the last cell under the "Instructors" heading, then choose Edit > Paste.

15 From the page, select "Jacob Dunn" and drag the text into the middle cell under "Instructors."

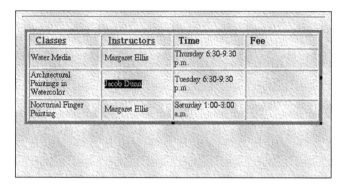

16 To finish the table, click in the first empty cell under the "Fee" heading and type **$475**. Type **$500** in the last two empty cells.

17 Delete the space left by the elements you moved into the table.

18 Choose File > Save Page.

Adding images to a table

You can also add images to a table. Since the Featured Student Work image is linked to a page featuring student work completed in classes, it makes sense to put this link inside the table. To create a space for it, you need to add a row at the bottom.

1 Click an insertion point anywhere in the first cell on the bottom row.

2 Drag the cursor to the lower right corner of the cell until you see a highlighted border surrounding the cell.

The highlighting indicates that the cell itself (but not the text inside it) is selected.

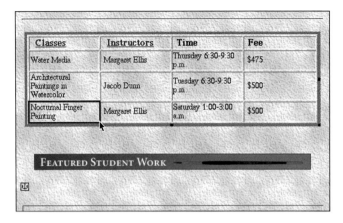

3 Click the Insert Row button (⬚) in the toolbar.

A new, empty row appears just below the one containing the selected cell.

4 Click on the page outside the table to deselect the cell you selected.

5 In the new row at the bottom, click an insertion point in the first cell. Drag the cursor all the way across the row to the last cell.

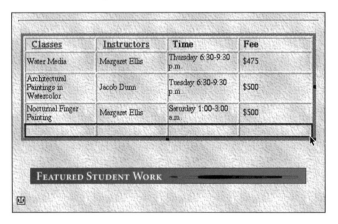

A highlighted border now surrounds all the cells in the last row, indicating that they are selected.

6 Click the Join Cells button (▭) in the toolbar.

The four cells are joined together to form one large cell. Now you'll add the image.

7 Beneath the table, select the Featured Student Work image, then drag it into the large table cell you just created. If there is extra space above the image, click an insertion point in the upper left corner of the cell and press Backspace to delete it.

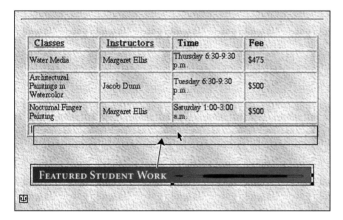

Note that the link for the image (indicated by the border) is preserved after placing it in the table.

By default, the images and text are aligned on the left of the cell. To center the contents of a cell, you need to use the Inspector. We'll center the contents of all the cells at once by selecting them all.

8 If the Inspector isn't open, choose View > Show Inspector (Windows) or Window > Show Inspector (MacOS).

9 In the table, click the upper left side of the cell that contains the Classes heading, then drag down to the lower right side of the table. All the cells in the table should now be selected and surrounded by a solid border.

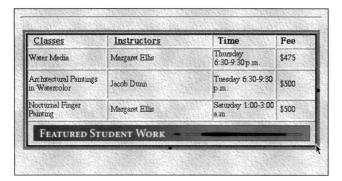

You'll also notice that the Inspector is displaying controls for adjusting table cells.

10 In the Inspector, select Center (Windows) or Middle (MacOS) in the Vertical Align section. Then select Center in the Horizontal Align section.

The contents of all the cells are now centered.

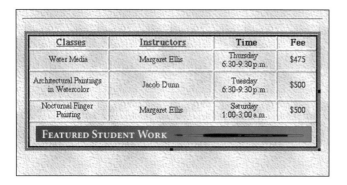

Making adjustments to a table

After you have created a table, you can adjust various attributes, including cell color and size. You'll set off the cells containing class information from the rest of the table by using a color.

1 If the table is still selected, click on the page outside the table to deselect it.

2 Click the upper left side of the cell that contains the Classes heading, then drag down and right to select all cells in the table except the one containing the Featured Student Work image.

As before, a single highlighted border surrounds the selected cells.

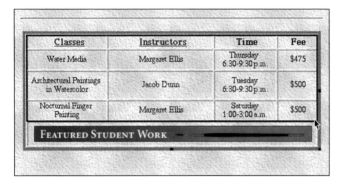

3 In the Inspector, choose Custom from the Background menu.

4 In the Color dialog box, select a pale blue color, then click OK.

The background of the selected cells changes to the selected color.

You can also change the border style for a table, specify thicker or thinner borders between cells, adjust the margins inside a cell, and add a caption to the table.

5 First, you need to display these controls in the Inspector. To do so, click on the very edge of the table so that a thin, solid border surrounds the table. If the table is surrounded by a thick, textured border, you've clicked inside the table instead of on its edge.

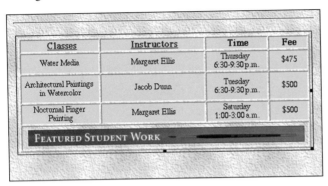

The Inspector now displays the following controls:

- The Border control adjusts the width of the border surrounding the table.

- The Cell Spacing control adjusts the width of borders between cells.

- The Cell Padding control adjusts the margin inside each cell.

6 Type **3** for Border, **2** for Cell Spacing, and **3** for Cell Padding. Press Enter or Return after each entry.

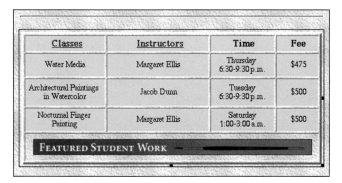

You can experiment with different values to see how the table changes. Entering 0 for Border turns off the border in a table, letting you use a table as a way to lay out a page with different elements, which you'll do in the next section.

Finally, you'll add a caption to the table.

7 In the Inspector, select the Caption option, then click the button on top of the table graphic.

A caption appears above the table.

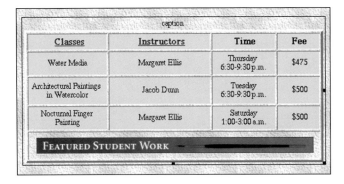

8 Double-click inside the table to switch to editing mode, select the word "Caption," and type **Curriculum**.

9 Select "Curriculum," choose Largest Heading from the Format menu in the toolbar, then click the Left Align Text button (≡) in the toolbar.

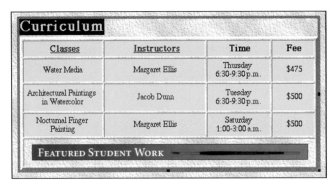

The table is finished!

10 Choose File > Save Page.

11 Switch to Preview mode to check the links.

Using a table to align images and text

You can also use a table to align an image with a block of text by turning off borders. Again, you'll rearrange some information on the Painting page.

1 Click the Preview icon to switch to Edit mode.

2 Scroll to the bottom of the PAINTING.HTM window to the section titled Instructors.

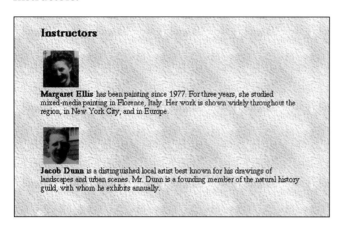

You'll find descriptions of the instructors with their photos underneath. You'll place the photos on the left and the descriptions on the right.

3 Click an insertion point to the right of the "Instructors" heading and press Enter or Return.

4 Instead of dragging the table button (⊞) to create the table, click the table button once.

A dialog box appears, providing controls for creating rows and columns.

5 Specify 2 rows and 2 columns, then click OK.

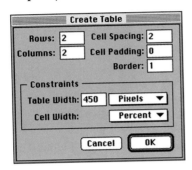

A 2x2 table appears.

6 Select the description for Margaret Ellis and drag it into the cell on the upper right.

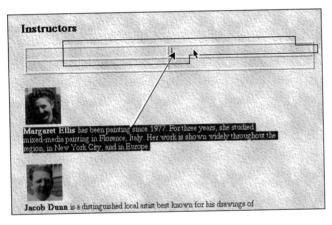

7 Select the description for Jacob Dunn and drag it into the cell on the lower right.

8 Now click the image of Margaret to select it and drag it into the cell on the upper left.

9 Select the image of Jacob and drag it into the cell on the lower left.

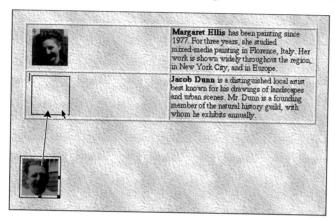

Now you'll bring the text closer to the images. You can adjust the size of cells by dragging the cell separators.

10 In the table, move the pointer over the vertical separator. When the pointer changes into a double arrow, drag the separator to the left until it comes close to (but doesn't touch) the images.

Finally, you'll touch up the table and remove the borders.

11 Select the table by clicking on the very edge of the table. A thin, solid line should surround the table.

12 In the Inspector, set the Border to 0, and Cell Spacing and Cell Padding to 2. Be sure to press Enter or Return after each entry.

13 Below the table, delete the remaining space between the table and the link "return to top."

14 To view the new layout, click the Edit icon to switch to Preview mode.

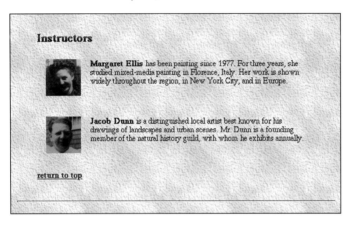

15 Choose File > Save Page, then close the PAINTING.HTM window.

Review questions

1 What are two ways to create a table?

2 What are three ways to add linked text or images to a table?

3 How do you make one table cell out of two?

4 How do you lay out text and images on a page?

Answers

1 You can drag the Table button to create a table with the desired number of columns and rows, or you can click the Table button to display the Create Table dialog box and then specify the number of columns and rows.

2 To add linked text or images to a table, you can drag them to a table cell, copy and paste them into a cell, or type text in a cell and link it.

3 Select the table so you can edit it, click an insertion point in the first cell and drag to a corner of the other cell until a border surrounds both cells, then click the Join Cells button in the toolbar.

4 Use a table to align text and images, dragging the vertical and horizontal separators as desired to move the text and images closer or farther apart. Then use the Inspector to set the cell spacing and padding and to remove the border.

Lesson 6

Creating a Form

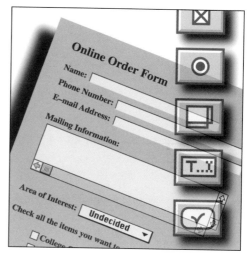

Web pages can be designed as online forms

that collect and record data entered by visitors

to the Web site.

In addition to providing interaction with links, Web pages can also include online forms that record data entered by visitors to the site, then send the data to the server for collection. In this lesson you'll lay out an order form—complete with menus and radio buttons— which potential students of the Art Academy can fill out on-screen and immediately send to the college.

Setting up the form controls and options on the page is easy. To record and send the data that the reader enters, a form requires a Common Gateway Interface (CGI) script written in a script or programming language, such as AppleScript® or Perl.

When the visitor presses the button that sends the data to the server, the server processes the data according to the script. A script can simply send the contents of the form somewhere, or perform more complex tasks, such as collecting the data into a database or generating a new page based on the form's content. In PageMill, you can create one form per page. Otherwise, the options are limited only by the capabilities of the scripting language.

Specific information about programming CGI scripts is outside the scope of this lesson, but there are many sources for CGI information on the World Wide Web. You can also consult your Webmaster for information about CGI script program-mers in your area.

In this lesson, you'll learn to:

• Create a form with a variety of form elements

• Associate a CGI script with a form to handle the data

Creating and naming the order form document

As you learned in Lesson 1, a new document, unlike an existing document, opens in Edit mode so you can begin working immediately.

1 Start PageMill. An untitled document opens in Edit mode.

If PageMill is already running, choose File > New Page to display an untitled document.

Notice that the Page-link icon on the left side of the toolbar is unavailable. You must save the document to make the Page-link icon available. First you'll add a heading and a page title before you save and name this page.

2 In the Title text box in the toolbar, type **Art Academy Order Form**. Press Enter or Return.

3 At the top of the page, type **Online Order Form,** then press Enter or Return.

4 Click in the paragraph you just typed and choose Larger Heading from the Format menu.

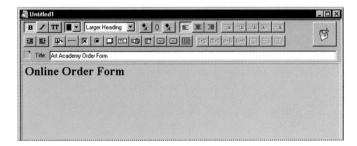

5 Choose File > Save Page.

6 In the dialog box, locate and open the Lesson6 folder in the WEBSITE folder.

7 Type **ORDER.HTM** for the filename and click Save. Be sure to use uppercase letters.

Adding and modifying text fields and text areas

You'll start with a straightforward form element, the text field. First you'll add the paragraphs that constitute the first section of the form, and then you'll add and modify the form elements.

1 Click an insertion point below the text "Online Order Form" and type the following items, pressing Enter or Return after each entry, except the last:

Name:

Phone Number:

E-mail Address:

Mailing Information:

Area of Interest:

Do not press Enter or Return after typing "Area of Interest."

If you make a typing error, you can backspace or use the arrow keys on your keyboard to move through the text.

2 Select the five paragraphs you just typed.

3 Choose Small Heading from the Format menu.

4 Click after the text "Name:".

5 In the toolbar, click the Insert Text Field button (T.I).

The text field appears at the default size.

6 Click to select the text field.

As you saw earlier with images and rules, you can select a form element to resize it. With this particular form element, however, you can only resize horizontally.

7 Select the handle on the right end of the text field, and drag it to the right a small amount to enlarge the field.

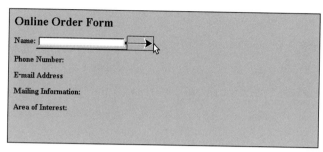

Now you'll duplicate the object.

8 Hold down Ctrl (Windows) or Option (MacOS), drag the field down, then release the mouse button when the insertion point appears after the text "Phone number:".

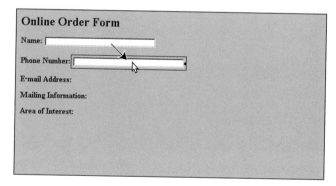

9 Hold down Ctrl or Option, drag the text field down, and release the mouse button when the insertion point appears after the text "E-mail address:".

Now you'll add a similar field called a Text Area, useful for containing larger amounts of text than a Text Field, which is limited to one line of text.

10 Click an insertion point at the end of the "Mailing Information" paragraph, and press Enter or Return.

11 Click the Insert Text Area button (▱) in the toolbar.

12 Click to select the text area.

13 Drag the handle on the right side to the right so that the edge of the box approximately aligns with the right edge of the E-mail Address text field.

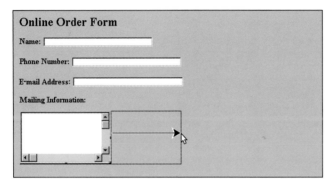

Adding a menu

The form elements you have added so far allow the visitor to the site to type in information. Now you'll add an element that asks the visitor to select from a set of choices.

1 Click an insertion point after the text "Area of Interest."

2 Click the Insert Pop-up button (▭) in the toolbar.

The placeholder text for the first menu option appears in the box.

3 With the insertion point to the right of the menu, press Enter or Return twice. This adds some space to separate the next section.

Now you'll edit the menu so that it lists the choices you want to make available.

4 Double-click the menu.

A border surrounds the element, indicating that you can edit its content.

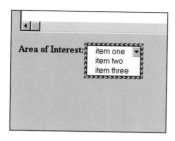

5 Choose Edit > Select All.

6 Type the following items, pressing Enter or Return after each word, except the last, to create new entries in the menu:

Design

Painting

Photography

Drawing

Undecided

Do not press Enter or Return after typing "Undecided."

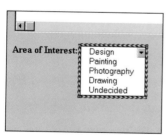

If you make a typing error, you can backspace or use the arrow keys on your keyboard to move through the text.

You can even drag and drop selected text. Now you'll alphabetize the list using the drag-and-drop method.

7 Double-click the word "Drawing" to select it.

The word becomes selected. You can also triple-click to select a menu option that uses multiple words.

8 Drag the selected text until the insertion point appears at the start of the word "Painting," then release the mouse button.

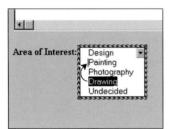 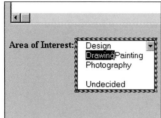

9 Click between the two words ("Painting" and "Drawing") and press Enter or Return.

10 Delete the space between "Photography" and "Undecided".

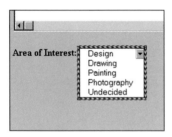

11 Click to the right of the menu to deselect it.

The menu automatically collapses to show only the first option.

Since the first option in the list might not be the option you want selected by default, PageMill lets you select any option to appear in the menu as it initially displays on the page.

12 Double-click the menu to revise its contents.

13 Drag the triangle icon on the right edge of the menu to the "Undecided" option.

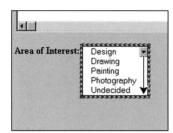 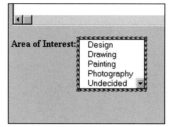

14 Click to the right of the menu to deselect it.

Now the "Undecided" option is selected by default.

Adding Checkboxes

In this section, you want to let the person filling out the form select any number of options available, which you can't do with a menu. Checkboxes are useful for this purpose.

1 Click an insertion point to the right of the menu if it is not there already, and press Enter or Return twice.

2 In the toolbar, click the Insert Horizontal Rule button (—), then press Enter or Return.

3 Type **Check all the items you want to receive:** and then press Enter or Return.

4 Click the Indent Right button (⁺⊐), and type the following items, pressing Enter or Return after each entry except the last one:

College Catalog

Application Packet

Scholarship Packet

Local Gallery and Museum Guide

Do not press Enter or Return after "Local Gallery and Museum Guide."

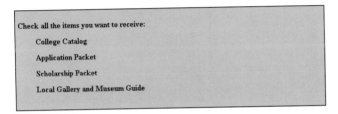

The indent helps to set off the checkboxes that you'll add in the next step.

5 Click at the start of the "College Catalog" paragraph, and click the Insert Checkbox button (⊠) in the toolbar.

6 Insert a checkbox at the start of each remaining paragraph, using either the Insert Checkbox button as in step 5, or by holding down Ctrl or Option as you drag and drop copies of the first checkbox you inserted.

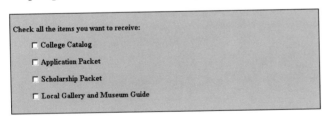

7 Choose File > Save Page.

Adding radio buttons

For the next section of the form you'll add a group of radio buttons. Radio buttons let you select one choice from a list of several possible choices. In other words, you can select just one button at a time.

1 Click an insertion point to the right of the text "Local Gallery and Museum Guide," and press Enter or Return.

2 Click the Indent Left button (⊏•).

3 Type the following text:

Intended Start Date:

Fall

Winter

Spring

Summer

4 To indent the list, select the four options you just typed ("Fall" through "Summer"), and click the Indent Right button in the toolbar.

5 Click an insertion point at the start of the word "Fall," then click the Insert Radio Button (⊙) in the toolbar.

The first radio button appears.

To group radio buttons so that only one of them can be selected at a time, you must duplicate the buttons rather than create new ones using the Insert Radio button in the toolbar. You'll duplicate the first button in the next step.

6 Hold down Ctrl or Option and drag the radio button from the start of the "Fall" paragraph to the start of the "Winter" paragraph below it.

A duplicate appears.

7 Hold down Ctrl or Option and drag either radio button you created to the start of the "Spring" paragraph.

8 Hold down Ctrl or Option and drag any one of the other radio buttons you created to the start of the "Summer" paragraph.

Once you've grouped radio buttons, you need to choose the one that will be selected when the user first sees them. You'll make Fall the choice that's initially selected.

9 Double-click the "Fall" radio button.

10 Click in the button so that it becomes black.

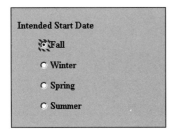

The button that had been selected becomes deselected. The Fall button now appears selected when the user first sees the page.

11 Click at the end of the paragraph "Summer," then press Enter or Return.

The radio button section is complete and you are ready to create the final section.

Adding Submit and Reset buttons

Every form you create is going to need a Submit button, a way for the visitor to send the information contained in the completed form to a server that collects it. In addition, a Reset button offers the user a fast way to clear the information that was entered without sending it anywhere.

Note that Submit and Reset buttons only work when you have associated the form with a CGI script. You'll do that later in the lesson.

1 Choose Format > Indent Left.

2 Click the Insert Horizontal Rule button (—)in the toolbar and press Enter or Return.

3 Click the Insert Submit Button (⌾) in the toolbar and press Enter or Return.

4 Click the Insert Reset Button (⌧) in the toolbar and press Enter or Return.

5 Click the Insert Horizontal Rule button again and press Enter or Return.

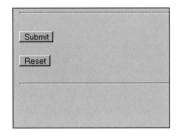

6 Double-click the Submit button.

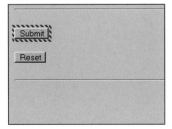

A border surrounds the button. As with other form elements, the border indicates that you can edit the text inside the element.

7 Select the text "Submit," type **Send Form,** and then click to the right of the button.

8 Double-click the Reset button.

9 Select the text "Reset," type **Start Over,** then click to the right of the button.

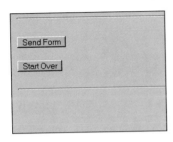

10 Choose File > Save Page.

Previewing the Form

You have entered all the form elements you need. In Preview mode, you can use the form as would a visitor to the Web site, and in that way determine whether the form is ready to be published. Note that in PageMill you cannot press Tab to move from one field to the next, as you can when the page is displayed in a Web browser. In addition, the Send Form (Submit) button does not send information and Start Over (Reset) does not clear entries.

After you preview your work, you'll come back and link the form to the rest of the Art Academy Web site.

1 Click the Edit icon to switch to Preview mode.

2 Complete the form as if filling it out for yourself.

Even though you are in Preview mode, you can type in the form and select options from the menu—the changes you make are cleared when you return to Edit mode. This lets you get a feel for how the form interacts with visitors to the Web site.

3 When you are through previewing the form, click the Preview icon to return to Edit mode.

Notice that returning to Edit mode resets the form automatically. If a text field is selected, click in a blank area on the page to deselect the text field.

Associating a CGI action script with a form

When a reader clicks Submit, the browser sends the data for every option and text field on the form to the Web server. For every form you create, you or your script programmer must provide a script on the server that handles the data.

In this section, you'll learn how to associate a script with a form. For the script to work correctly, however, the script must recognize the names and values it receives from the form objects on your page. For this you would have to work with a CGI script programmer to make sure that the names and values of your form objects are consistent with those in the script. For more information about CGI scripts, see Chapter 8, "Creating Forms" in the *Adobe Pagemill 2.0 User Guide.*

1 If necessary, choose View > Show Inspector (Windows) or Window > Show Inspector (MacOS).

2 In the Inspector, click the Form icon (▭).

Now you'll type the pathname of the Web server to which the form sends data.

3 In the Inspector, click an insertion point in the Action text box and type the following pathname:

http://www.artacademy.edu/cgi-bin/order.cgi

For your own forms, you would get the actual pathname to the script from your Internet Service Provider or Webmaster.

4 Press Enter or Return. In the menu below the Action text box, make sure Post is selected.

The Get and Post options specify how data entered into the form is sent to the server. The Get option appends the data to the end of the specified URL. The Post option assembles the data into a "packet" so the server knows exactly when the data starts and ends.

In most cases, the Post option is preferred, but the option you choose for your own forms will depend on the type of server and how the CGI script is written. You would consult with your script programmer to determine which option is best.

Linking the form to the Home and Admissions page

At this point, there's no way for a visitor to the Web site to get to the order form page. You'll add those links in this section.

1 Choose File > Open, then double-click the ADMISSNS.HTM file in the Lesson6 folder.

2 Click the Preview icon to switch to Edit mode.

3 Choose Window > Tile Vertically (Windows) or Window > Tile (MacOS) to view the Order page and the Admissions page side by side.

4 In the ADMISSNS.HTM window, scroll until you find the "For More Information" bulleted item, then click it to jump to that section of the page.

5 In the section For More Information on the Admissions page, scroll down, if necessary, to the paragraph beginning with the bold text "Online order form." Select the italicized text "Click here" as the source of the link. In the next step, you'll drag the destination onto this text, so a visitor to the site can quickly go to the form.

6 Drag the Page-link icon (□) from the ORDER.HTM window to the text selected in the ADMISSNS.HTM window.

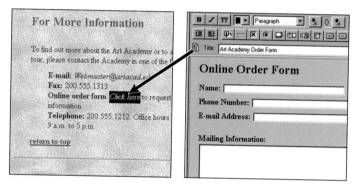

The link is established from the Admissions page to the order form.

7 In the ORDER.HTM window, scroll down, if necessary, to make sure the Send Form and Start Over buttons are in view.

8 Click an insertion point below the horizontal rule beneath the buttons. You do not need to press Enter or Return.

9 Click the Place Object button (⌷) in the toolbar. In the IMAGES folder in the Lesson6 folder, select ADRETURN.GIF and click Place.

10 Select the Admissions image you just placed.

11 Drag the Page-link icon from the ADMISSNS.HTM window onto the selected Admissions image on the Order page.

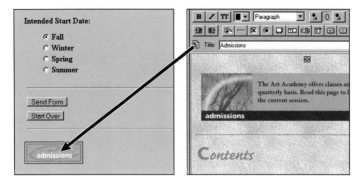

12 Click in a blank area on the page to deselect the image.

13 In the ADMISSNS.HTM window, select the "Return Home" image, which links back to the home page.

14 Drag the image to the ORDER.HTM window, and when the insertion point appears to the right of the Admissions image, release the mouse button.

15 If necessary, click the ADMISSNS.HTM window to make it active, then choose File > Save Page. Close the ADMISSNS.HTM window.

The links to and from the page are now complete. To finish, you'll add a few visual improvements to the Order page.

16 Expand the ORDER.HTM window, if necessary, then choose Edit > Select All and Format > Indent Right to create space on the left side of the page.

17 Click anywhere in the window to deselect the text and images.

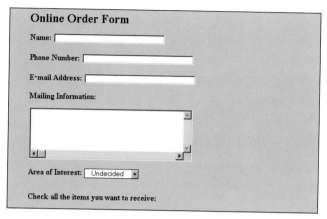

18 In the Inspector, click the Page tab (▢) if it is not already selected, and from the Background menu, choose Custom.

19 In the color dialog box, select a tan or dark yellow color for the background.

20 Click OK to close the dialog box, then close the Inspector so you can see the page clearly.

The page is ready for the Web.

21 Choose File > Save Page, then close the ORDER.HTM window.

Review questions

1 How do you add several text fields of equal length to a form?

2 How do you change the default option in a form menu?

3 How does the functionality of radio buttons differ from that of checkboxes?

4 What does a Reset button do?

5 Why is a CGI script necessary?

Answers

1 Click the Insert Text Field button in the toolbar to add the first text field and resize it. Then duplicate the text field by holding down Ctrl (Windows) or Option (MacOS) while you drag the text field to another location. Drag either of the text fields to create another one of equal length.

2 Double-click the form menu so you can revise its contents, then drag the triangle-icon on the right edge of the menu to the new option.

3 Radio buttons let you select one button at a time, whereas checkboxes let you select any number of options available.

4 If a form has been associated with a CGI script, then pressing a Reset button clears the information entered in the form without sending it anywhere.

5 A CGI script enables the Web server to accept and store the information in the form.

Lesson 7

Creating an Image Map

Image maps can greatly enhance a Web page by letting you include links in different parts of a single image. In this way, parts of the image can act as buttons.

In previous lessons, you learned that either text or graphics can link to a destination. But in this lesson, you'll see that a single image can include multiple links (or clickable hot spots) to different destinations. When a single image in a Web page includes one or more linked hot spots within it, the image is called an image map.

In this lesson, you'll learn to:

• Add hot spots to an image

• Link hot spots on an image to destinations

• Create an invisible border on a hot spot

Internal and external image maps

PageMill lets you create two different kinds of image maps: an internal map and an external map. When you create an internal (client-side) image map, PageMill places the information about the links inside the Web page you are editing. When you create an external (server-side) image map, that same information is placed in a separate file, called a .MAP file.

Other than files, what's the difference between the two kinds of image maps? Internal maps are simpler and more efficient, but not all Web browsers support them. (Both Netscape Navigator 2.0 or later and all versions of Microsoft Internet Explorer support them). On the other hand, external maps must communicate with the Web server using a CGI script, relaying link information back and forth as a user clicks on hot spots. This process may be time-consuming, creating delays in displaying and downloading information. The only major advantage to creating external image maps is that they are supported by all Web browsers. (For more information on server-side image maps, see the *Adobe PageMill 2.0 User Guide*.)

Adding hot spots to an image

You can make any image in your document an image map by adding hot spots. Hot spots can be any shape or size, and you can have any number of them on the same image.

In this lesson, you'll create an internal image map by adding hot spots to the Art Academy logo at the top of the Home page from Lesson 1. The first step, though, is to open the documents you will be linking to.

1 Start PageMill, if necessary, then close the Untitled window.

2 Choose File > Open, locate and open the Lesson7 folder in the WEBSITE folder, then double-click the HOME.HTM file.

In addition to the links you created to the Admissions and Offerings sections, the Home page now includes links to the Events and Tour sections of the Web site.

3 In the HOME.HTM window, click the Preview icon to switch to Edit mode.

4 Double-click the Art Academy logo at the top of the Home page to select it.

A thick textured border appears around the selected image, and the drawing tools appear in the second line of the toolbar . Two hot spots, "Tour" and Events," have already been created. You'll use the polygon tool to create the remaining two hot spots.

Note: You can use any of the three drawing tools to create hot spots for an image map.

5 Click the polygon tool (△) in the toolbar. This tool creates a hot spot of any shape using straight lines, but works a little differently than the other two drawing tools. You'll draw a four-sided shape around the Offerings section.

6 Drag the cross hair from the bottom left corner of the Offerings section up along the edge of the blue area. At the top of the blue area, click the mouse button to complete one line segment.

7 Now drag the cross hair to the right, then down, and finally to the left around the word "offerings," clicking the mouse button each time you change direction.

8 To complete the shape, you can do one of the following:

• Click the last line segment so that it connects to the start of the first line segment.

• Double-click to let PageMill automatically connect the first line segment to the last line segment.

  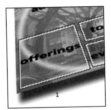

If you make a mistake, double-click to end the line segment, press Delete, then begin again.

Now you'll draw the second hot spot.

9 Click the polygon tool again, and draw a four-sided shape around the Admissions section.

Now that you've created the hot spots, you need to link each of them to their destinations. You'll start with the link to the Admissions page.

Linking hot spots in an image map

You link hot spots in an image map just as you do other text or images—by dragging a Page-link icon or anchor onto the hot spot.

1 In the HOME.HTM window, click the Edit icon to switch to Preview mode.

2 Scroll down to the navigation bar, if necessary, and position the pointer on the linked text "Admissions."

3 Hold down the mouse button. (In Windows, use the right mouse button.)

4 In the small menu, choose New Window, then release the mouse button.

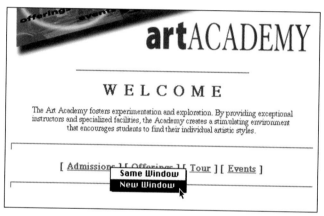

The Admissions page appears in a separate window. This page is the destination for the first link.

5 Choose Window > Tile Vertically (Windows) or Window > Tile (MacOS) to place the windows side by side.

6 Click the HOME.HTM window to make it active, then click the Preview icon to switch to Edit mode.

7 Drag the Page-link icon from the toolbar in the ADMISSNS.HTM window to the "admissions" hot spot in the Art Academy logo. When the hot spot is highlighted, release the mouse button.

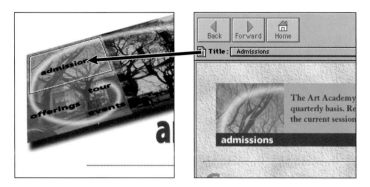

The title of the Admissions page now appears in the hot spot, indicating that the hot spot is linked to the page.

8 If necessary, click the ADMISSNS.HTM window to make it active, then close the window.

Now you'll repeat these steps for the next hot spot, "offerings."

9 In the HOME.HTM window, click the Edit icon to switch to Preview mode.

10 In the navigation bar, hold down the mouse button (right mouse button in Windows) on the linked text "Offerings," and choose New Window.

The Offerings page appears in a separate window. This page is the destination for the next link.

11 If necessary, choose Window > Tile Vertically (Windows) or Window > Tile (MacOS) to place the windows side by side, then click the Preview icon in the HOME.HTM window to switch to Edit mode.

12 Drag the Page-link icon from the toolbar in the OFFERING.HTM window to the "offerings" hot spot on the Art Academy logo. When the hot spot is highlighted, release the mouse button.

13 Close the OFFERING.HTM window, and maximize the HOME.HTM window, if necessary.

Again, the link information appears in the hot spot.

Next you'll link the next hot spot by typing the name of the destination file. Ordinarily you should avoid typing link information—a single typo can invalidate the link—but in this case the filename is straightforward enough that you'll have no problems.

1 Click the "tour" hot spot to select it.

2 In the Link To bar at the bottom of the HOME.HTM window, type **TOUR.HTM** and press Enter or Return. Be sure to type the filename exactly as shown, using uppercase letters.

The link is established and the destination filename appears within the hot spot.

For the last hot spot, you'll save some typing by copying the last link.

3 Double-click to select the "Events" link in the navigation bar.

4 Now drag the Globe icon in the lower left corner of the window onto the last hot spot, "events."

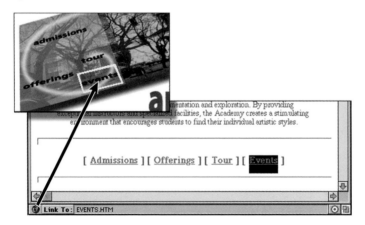

You've copied the same link information from the "Events" link.

The link is established and the destination filename appears in the hot spot.

Assigning the map attribute to the image

Now you'll tell PageMill to treat the image as a map rather than as a static picture. Then you'll be ready to test the links.

1 If the hot spots are still outlined in the Art Academy logo on the Home page, click anywhere on the page outside the image to deselect them.

2 Now click once on the image to select it.

3 If the Inspector isn't visible, choose View > Show Inspector (Windows) or Window > Show Inspector (MacOS).

4 Make sure the Object tab (▪) and the Map option are selected, and the Border is set to 0.

A border of zero pixels prevents a Web browser from adding a band of color (usually blue) around the image map to indicate the image is linked. There might be instances where you want the link indicator to appear, but in this case it would detract from the overall page design.

5 Close the Inspector.

6 Choose File > Save Page.

Testing the image map

Now you can test the image map to make sure the links work correctly. You can test the links in either PageMill or in a Web browser. You'll use the Web browser.

1 In the HOME.HTM window, choose View > Switch To (Windows) or Window > Switch To (MacOS), then select a Web browser.

The Home page appears in the browser.

2 Move the cursor over the Admissions section of the Art Academy logo, and when the cursor becomes a pointing hand, click the link.

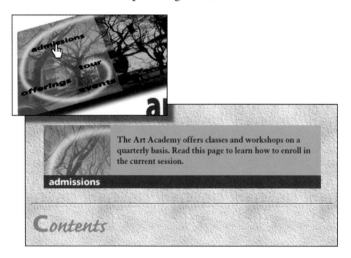

The Admissions page appears.

3 In the Web browser, click the Back button.

4 Now click the "Offerings" section of the Art Academy logo image.

The Offerings page appears.

5 Repeat steps 3 and 4 with the other two links.

6 Close the Web browser window.

7 In PageMill, choose Window > Close All.

Review questions

1 How do internal image maps differ from external ones?

2 Which tools can you use to draw hot spots for an image map?

3 What are three ways to link a hot spot on an image map to a page in a Web site?

4 How do you remove the link-indicator border from a linked object?

Answers

1 Internal image maps are faster because all link information is stored inside the Web page. In an external map, the link information is placed in a separate file and stored on a Web server, where the process of displaying and downloading information can be time-consuming. However, not all Web browsers support internal image maps.

2 You can use three tools, including the polygon, rectangle, and circle.

3 You can do any of the following:

• Drag the Page-link icon from the destination page to the hot spot.

• Select an object or text with the same link, then drag the Globe icon (next to the Link To bar) onto the hot spot in the image map.

• Select the hot spot and enter the destination filename in the Link To bar at the bottom of the PageMill window.

4 Select the linked object. Then, in the Inspector, set the Border to 0.

Lesson 8
Using Frames

Frames can enhance the look of your Web site while also providing easier ways for users to find and follow links.

In previous lessons, clicking a link to another page in the Art Academy site displayed that page in one of two ways:

- The new page was displayed in the same window, replacing the window's current contents.
- The new page was displayed in a new and separate window.

Frames give you a third option. They let you display a link on a portion of a page, while keeping the rest of the page the same. In general, frames give you more control over the way users navigate and see information in your Web site. In this lesson, you'll learn to:

- Create a frame
- Target a link from one frame to another frame
- Save a frameset

About frames

A frame is a portion of a Web page, separated from the rest of the page by a border.

Frame files and their associated frames

Frames visually divide a window into different areas, with each frame displaying information independently of the other areas. For this reason, the contents of each frame must be saved as a separate file. For example, if you have divided a page into three frames, you must save three different files to display different information in each frame. When a Web browser displays a page that has been separated into frames, it must load the files into the frames.

But how does the Web browser know which file to load into each frame? In addition to saving files for each frame, you must also save a frameset file. The frameset file contains formatting information, such as frame size, frame border, and the name of the file to be displayed in each frame.

Using frames

Frames visually divide information on a page into these distinct areas, separated by borders:

Navigation   One frame contains a list of links, while another displays a link when it is clicked. In this way, users can more easily navigate through a series of pages. You'll create a navigation frame for one of the tours.

Fixed information   If you want to prevent an element, such as a banner, from scrolling, you can create a frame for it. Users can scroll the rest of the page, but the banner always remains visible. You'll create a banner frame for the tour page.

Updated information   Frequently updated areas of a page, such as advertising space or hourly announcements, can be placed in separate frames. The remainder of the page remains unchanged.

Creating frames

You can create frames either on a new, empty page or on one that already has content. You'll start with one of the Tour pages to see how you can rearrange information into frames.

1 Start PageMill, if necessary, then close the Untitled window.

2 Choose File > Open, locate and open the Lesson8 folder in the WEBSITE folder, then double-click the CAMPUS.HTM file.

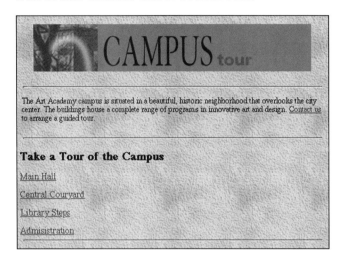

This page provides a tour of art studios with links for each studio. Unlike the tour you created in Lesson 4, which used anchors in one file, links in this tour each open a separate page.

As you've seen in other lessons, clicking on each link replaces the contents of the page and displays the new one. In this lesson, you'll change how the links work by making them display on the same page, in a different frame.

First, you'll create a frame for the banner at the top of the CAMPUS.HTM page.

3 Click the Preview icon in the upper right corner of the page to switch to Edit mode.

4 In the CAMPUS.HTM window, hold down Ctrl (Windows) or Option (MacOS), then position the pointer over the thin line that forms the top border of the editing area, just below the toolbar.

Note that the pointer changes to a small arrow (↓). If it doesn't, make sure you're placing the pointer exactly on the thin line.

5 While holding down Ctrl or Option, drag the small arrow down the page, between the banner image and the first horizontal rule.

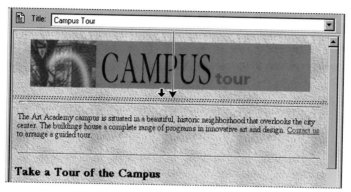

An empty area appears in the upper portion of the window with a horizontal and vertical scroll bar. This area is a frame. Note that you are no longer editing the CAMPUS.HTM file. Instead, you have created a new document which has CAMPUS.HTM loaded into one of its frames.

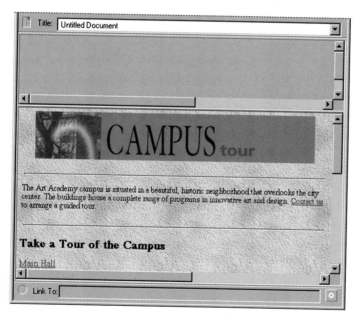

Note how the content on the rest of the page has been pushed downward to make room for the frame. This content is actually contained in a second frame, since you've separated the page into two frames—upper and lower. Each frame acts as a separate window, displaying the content you specify. You can place content into a frame just as you can for any page.

Now you'll rearrange the page and put some content into the upper frame.

6 In the lower frame, select the "Campus Tour" banner, then choose Edit > Cut.

7 Click in the upper frame to select it. The border of the frame is now highlighted.

8 Choose Edit > Paste. The Campus Tour banner appears in the upper frame. If the frame covers part of the image, don't worry; you'll adjust the frame height in a later step.

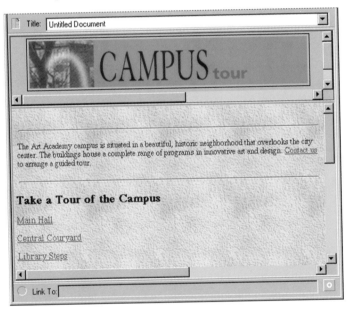

The banner is now fixed at the top of the page; users can scroll other frames, but the banner does not move, always remaining visible.

The upper frame still has a horizontal and a vertical scroll bar. PageMill lets you turn scroll bars on or off in each frame, depending on your preferences or the amount of content in the frame. Since the upper frame does not need scroll bars, you'll turn them off.

9 If the upper frame is not still selected, click in it (but don't click the banner).

10 If the Inspector is not visible, choose View > Show Inspector (Windows) or Window > Show Inspector (MacOS).

11 If necessary, click the Frame tab (⊞) in the Inspector.

12 In the Inspector, find the Scrollbars menu and choose No. The Inspector provides a number of different controls for adjusting a frame. For now, you'll just use this one.

Notice that the upper frame no longer has scroll bars. Now you can adjust the height of the frame, if needed.

To adjust a frame manually, you place the pointer on a border of a frame. When the pointer changes to a double-headed arrow, you can drag the frame border up or down. Another way to adjust the frame is by entering an exact pixel size, which you'll do next.

13 In the Inspector, choose Pixels from the Height menu, then type **93** in the text box next to the menu. Press Enter or Return. The frame adjusts to fit the Campus Tour banner.

Now you'll add a tiled background to the frame.

14 If necessary, click in the upper frame (but not on the banner) to select the frame.

15 In the Inspector, click the Page tab (▢) to display page controls.

Remember that because a frame acts as a page, you have all the page controls available for a frame.

16 In the Inspector, click File at the bottom of the palette (Windows) or the File icon (▢) (MacOS), then double-click the TOURTILE.GIF file in the Images folder in the Lesson8 folder.

That's it! You've successfully created your first frame.

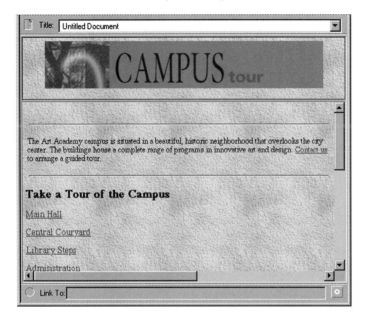

As mentioned before, the content in each frame must be saved as a file. A Web browser loads a file into each frame when the page is first displayed. Since you're finished with the frame that contains the banner, you'll save it.

17 If necessary, click in the upper frame to select it.

18 Choose File > Save Page (Windows) or File > Save Frame (MacOS).

19 Locate and open the FRAMES folder in the Lesson8 folder. Then type **BANNER.HTM** in uppercase letters for the filename and click Save.

Note that the window still says "Untitled." That's because you haven't yet saved the frameset file. Once you create a frame on a page, the page becomes "Untitled," and must be saved as a frameset.

Saving the frameset

The frameset file contains information about the frames, including the filenames that are initially loaded into each frame. To match a frame with a file, the frameset file must keep track of both the filename and the frame name.

As the designer of the Web page, you must keep track of the filenames for each frame. In general, however, you can let PageMill keep track of frame names. Whenever you create a frame, it is automatically given a name, which consists of the word "frame" plus a number. You can view and change the frame name in the Inspector.

1 If necessary, click in the upper frame (but not on the banner) to select it.

2 If necessary, click the Frame tab (⊞) in the Inspector.

In the Inspector, the text box next to Name displays the default frame name. Although you can change this name, you can usually leave each frame with its default name, unless you are editing HTML code and need to use frame names to remember which frame displays which file. Otherwise, the frameset file remembers for you.

Important: Do not change frame names after you target links, or the Web browser will not display frame contents properly.

Now you'll name and save the layout and configuration of the frameset.

3 Choose File > Frameset > Save Frameset (Windows) or File > Save Frameset (MacOS). In the FRAMES folder in the Lesson8 folder, type **TOUR.HTM** in uppercase letters and click Save. The name in the title bar of the window changes to TOUR.HTM.

Targeting links in another frame

Now that you've created a simple, fixed frame, you can create a frame for navigation by targeting links in one frame to display in another. You'll rearrange the remaining information in the TOUR.HTM window to create a navigation frame.

1 In the lower frame of the TOUR.HTM window, position the pointer over the thin line that forms the border of the right side of the window.

2 Hold down Ctrl (Windows) or Option (MacOS), so that the pointer becomes a small arrow (◆), then drag the new frame to the right, about two thirds of the way across the page.

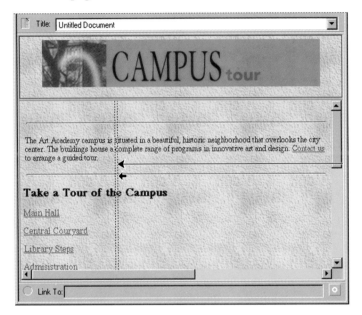

Note that the contents of the window have been resized to fit inside the narrow frame.

Instead of sizing the new frame by pixels, the way you did for the upper frame, you'll use a percent this time.

3 Click inside the lower left frame to select it.

4 In the Frame tab of the Inspector, make sure Percent is chosen from the Width menu, then type **35** in the text box next to the menu. Press Enter or Return.

The width of the frame is sized at 35 percent of the window's width, even if the window's width is changed. The percent width also applies to the frame when it's displayed in a Web browser.

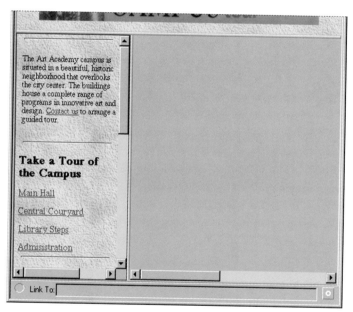

Now you'll center the contents in the frame you just created.

5 Click an insertion point anywhere in the lower left frame and choose Edit > Select All.

6 In the toolbar, click the Center Align Text button (≡).

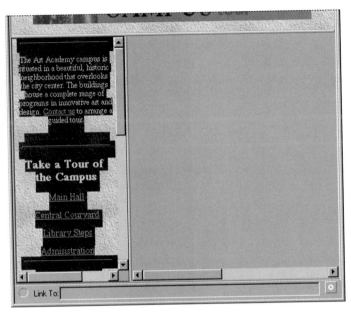

Since this frame contains information that goes beyond the length of the frame, you'll keep the scroll bars.

The tour hot spots have been linked to separate pages. Currently, these links, when clicked, will display the page in the same frame. This is the default behavior, but it's not what you want. You want the pages to display in the frame on the right. To do this, you must target the link.

7 In the lower left frame, triple-click the "Main Hall" link just beneath the heading, "Take a Tour of the Campus." The link appears in the Link To bar at the bottom of the window.

8 With the pointer over the "Main Hall" link, hold down the mouse button (use the right mouse button in Windows).

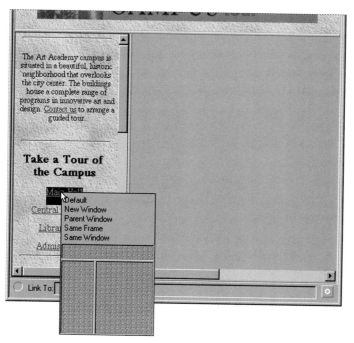

The target menu appears, providing various choices and also showing a representation of frames in the window. By moving the pointer across this representation, you can select a specific frame as a target for the link.

Holding down the mouse button on the target icon (⊙) in the lower right corner of the window displays the same target menu and frame representation.

9 Continue holding down the mouse button on the link and move the pointer to select the frame on the lower right. Release the mouse button.

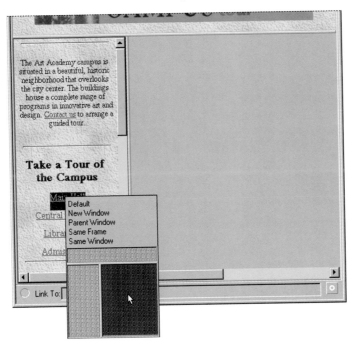

When a visitor clicks the "Main Hall" link, its contents will be displayed in the frame on the lower right. The frame containing the links will not change.

10 To display each section of the studio tour in the lower right frame, repeat the steps 7-9 for the other three links: "Central Courtyard," "Library Steps," and "Administration."

There are three more links on this page that you need to target: the "Studios" and "Gallery" links for the other tours, and the "Home Page" link. Although you could display these links in one of the frames on the current page, these links are meant to be displayed as full pages. So you'll target these links to display in the same window, replacing the current contents.

11 Select the "Studios" link and hold down the mouse button (right mouse button in Windows). Instead of selecting a target frame, choose the Same Window option from the menu.

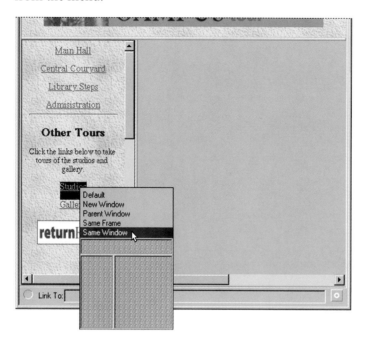

12 Repeat step 11 for the "Gallery" and "Return Home" links.

13 Save the frame by choosing File > Save Page As (Windows) or File > Save Frame As (MacOS). Locate the FRAMES folder in the Lesson8 folder, type **NAVIGATE.HTM** in uppercase letters for the filename, and click Save.

14 Choose File > Frameset > Save Frameset (Windows) or File > Save Frameset (MacOS) to save the layout and configuration of the frameset.

Finally, you'll finish the page by adding an image to the lower right frame, which is currently empty. This image will be displayed in the frame before the visitor starts the tour. First, you'll make the background black to set off all the graphics that will appear there.

15 Click inside the lower right frame to select it.

16 Choose View > Show Color Panel (Windows) or Window > Show Color Panel (MacOS).

17 If the Inspector isn't open, choose View > Show Inspector (Windows) or Window > Show Inspector (MacOS). Make sure both palettes are visible.

18 In the Inspector, click the Page tab ( ).

19 Drag the black circle from the Color Panel onto the Background menu in the Inspector. If you inadvertently drag the circle to the wrong menu, choose Edit > Undo (Windows) or Edit > Undo Background Color and drag the circle again.

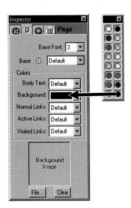

20 Click the Place Object button (⊞) in the toolbar, locate and open the Images folder in the Lesson8 folder, then double-click the CAMPUS.GIF file.

The Campus image appears in the frame. To adjust its position, you can specify a margin height and width for the frame.

21 In the Inspector, click the Frame tab (⊞).

22 Leave the Margin Width at 5, then type 15 for the Margin Height, and press Enter or Return.

23 Choose No from the Scrollbars menu.

24 Click the Center Align Text button in the toolbar.

25 Choose File > Save Page (Windows) or File > Save Frame (MacOS). In the FRAMES folder in the Lesson8 folder, type **INITIAL.HTM** in uppercase letters for the filename, then click Save.

The contents in the frame you just saved will be displayed when the page is first opened, but will be replaced when a visitor clicks on the tour hot spots.

You've completed the frames on this page.

26 Choose File > Frameset > Save Frameset (Windows) or File > Save Frameset (MacOS).

Here's a quick review of what you have accomplished with this page. You separated the page into three frames. For each of those frames you saved a file: BANNER.HTM, NAVIGATE.HTM, and INITIAL.HTM.

To tie them all together, you saved the frameset file, TOUR.HTM. That's a total of four files required for the page.

Now you'll check the links to make sure they display correctly.

27 Click the Edit icon to switch to Preview mode.

28 If necessary, maximize the window and close the palettes.

29 Click the first tour link, "Main Hall."

A photograph of the main hall should appear in the lower right frame.

30 Now click the other three tour links to display their contents in the same frame.

31 Finally, click the Return Home image to make sure that the Home page replaces the current page.

You've completed the lesson on using frames.

Review questions

1 How do frames help a visitor to the Web site navigate through a series of pages?

2 What are three ways to control the size of a frame?

3 What is a frameset, and why is it necessary?

4 How do you display the contents of a linked page in a separate frame?

Answers

1 The navigation links can stay in one frame, while the Web pages appear in a separate frame.

2 You can do any of the following:

- Hold down Ctrl (Windows) or Option (MacOS) and drag the border.

- Enter the number of pixels in the Inspector, with the Frame tab selected.

- Enter a percentage in the Inspector, with the Frame tab selected.

3 A frameset contains formatting information about each frame and the name of the file to be displayed in each frame. A frameset is necessary in order to match a frame with a file.

4 Select the link. Then hold down the mouse button (right-mouse button in Windows) and select an option from the target menu or drag the pointer to a specific frame.

Linking to External Resources

Documents on the Web can link to many different kinds of files, including movies, sounds, and pages on other Web sites.

Not only can PageMill link to HTML documents, it can link to other types of files, such as movies, sounds, or files in Adobe Acrobat Portable Document Format (PDF). PageMill can also link to Web pages that are outside your own Web site.

In this lesson you'll learn to:

• Download and view a PDF file

• Create links with both relative and absolute URLs

• Use the "mailto" URL to allow visitors to the Web site to send you electronic mail

• Copy links from the Web browser into PageMill

• Copy external links from one source to another

About PDF files

The first kind of file you'll link to is a document called a PDF file. PDF files can be created from just about any PostScript® file, using the Adobe Acrobat Distiller®. If you need sophisticated graphic design or layout on pages in your Web site, you'll probably want to create some of your pages asDF files. PDF files let you display any design that you can save as a PostScript file, using layouts and typographical characteristics that are not possible with HTML. But like HTML, PDF files also let you include hypertext links between pages and to the World Wide Web. In addition, you can load a multipage PDF document into the Web browser window.

The Art Academy Web site contains two PDF files:

• The PDF file on the Admissions page lets a potential applicant to the Art Academy download and then print the official application to the college—complete with the correct fonts and graphics embedded in the file.

• The PDF file on the Events page downloads and displays a design-intensive invitation created for on-screen viewing.

If you include PDF files, you should provide a link to the Adobe Acrobat Reader application, which is required to view PDF files. When the Web browser is used with the PDFViewer plug-in, clicking a link to a PDF file loads both the file and Acrobat Reader directly into the browser window.

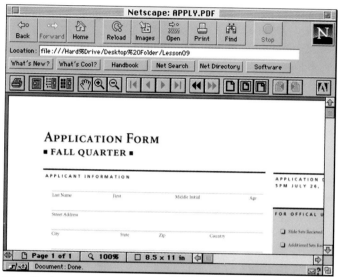

PDF file displayed in a Web browser.

For more information about PDF files and Adobe Acrobat, see the Adobe Web site at http://www.adobe.com.

Using Uniform Resource Locators (URLs)

A Uniform Resource Locator (URL) is an address that tells the Web browser where to find a page or file outside the local Web site. The external file can exist on a local hard disk, or on a hard disk thousands of miles away. Using Internet protocol and the URL you specified, the Web browser finds the file, downloads it, and displays it on-screen.

When linking to external files, you can specify either a relative URL or an absolute URL. A relative URL, which is usually short and easy to type, specifies a location of a file relative to the location of the page containing the link. Throughout previous lessons, you've been using relative URLs to link to other pages in the Art Academy site.

An absolute URL specifies the complete and unique address of a file, independent of all other files. If you are linking to a file on another volume or server, you must always specify an absolute URL.

In this lesson, you'll create links with both types of URLs.

Using a relative URL with a PDF file

You'll use a relative URL to download a PDF file.

1 Start PageMill, if necessary, then close the Untitled window.

2 Choose File > Open, locate and open the Lesson9 folder in the WEBSITE folder, then double-click the EVENTS.HTM file.

3 Scroll to the "Exhibition Schedule" link and click it to jump to that section of the page.

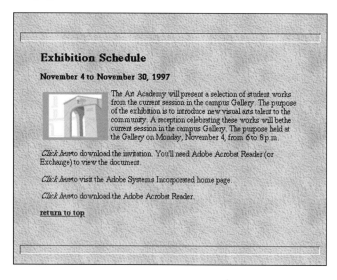

4 Click the Preview icon to switch to Edit mode.

As with any other kind of link, the first step is to select the source.

5 Select the text "Click here" in the sentence "Click here to download the invitation."

6 Click in the Link To bar at the bottom of the window.

7 Type **INVITE.PDF** and press Enter or Return.

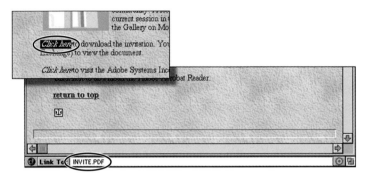

The link is established. Remember that you must press Enter or Return after specifying an address in the Link To bar.

The address you typed, which is simply a filename, is a relative URL —it is relative to the location of the EVENTS.HTM file. A Web browser can access the PDF document, provided the PDF file is stored in the same folder as EVENTS.HTM.

8 Choose File > Save Page.

Now you'll see how the PDF file looks when it's displayed in a Web browser. But first, make sure you're ready for this step. Your system must have at least 24 MB of free hard-disk space available to run all three applications: PageMill, the browser, and Acrobat Reader. Then make sure you have installed Acrobat Reader 3.0. For installation instructions, see on "Installing other software" on page 3.

9 Choose View > Switch To (Windows) or Window > Switch To (MacOS), then choose a Web browser.

10 Click the link "Click here" to download the Invitation in PDF format.

The browser now displays the PDF file inside the embedded Acrobat Reader application.

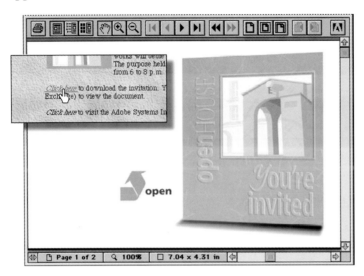

11 Read the second page of the invitation by using the scroll bar, clicking the forward arrow button at the top of the Reader window, or clicking the "open" link embedded in the PDF file.

12 Close the Web browser window.

Typing an absolute URL

You can specify an absolute URL in the same way you specified the relative URL. You'll create a link using the absolute URL to the Adobe home page.

1 Below the text you linked in the previous procedure, select the text "Click here" in the line "Click here to visit the Adobe Systems Incorporated home page."

2 In the Link To bar, type the following address, or see the tip below:

http://www.adobe.com

In PageMill, the Tab key and forward arrow on the keyboard act as shortcuts to typing the link, and also help to prevent typing errors. You can use either key to fill in the parts of a URL that are uniformly named across the Internet. For example, in the URL for the Adobe home page, you can type just the "h" in "http" and press Tab or the arrow key. PageMill fills in the rest of that part of the URL. This technique works for "www" and "com" as well.

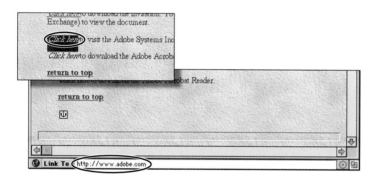

3 Press Enter or Return.

When visitors to the Web site click this link, they'll go directly to the Adobe home page.

4 Choose File > Save Page.

When you set the external link preference in the Introduction section of this book, you specified a Web browser. By setting this preference, you can click on an external link in Preview mode to automatically start the Web browser.

5 Click the Edit icon to switch to Preview mode.

Note: You must be connected to the Internet for the next step to work.

6 Click the link "Click here" in the line "Click here to visit the Adobe Systems Incorporated home page."

The Web browser starts and displays the Adobe home page. The Adobe home page changes frequently, so it probably won't match the illustrations in this book.

Dragging a URL from a Web browser

You can also specify an absolute URL by dragging it directly from a page in a Web browser onto a selected link in PageMill. You'll create a link to the Web page where Adobe makes Acrobat Reader available. First, you'll include the Adobe official Get Acrobat Reader button.

Note: You are free to use the Get Acrobat Reader button on your own Web page, but you must first fill out a form available online from Adobe.

1 In the EVENTS.HTM window in PageMill, click the Preview icon to switch to Edit mode.

2 Arrange the EVENTS.HTM window and the Adobe home page so both are visible.

3 Click the title bar of the Adobe home page to make it active, then find the Get Acrobat Reader button.

Dragging linked text or images from a Web page is not quite the same as dragging an image file from a folder because the dragging action must be more swift and smooth from the Web page. For example, if you click and hold a linked image on a Web page before dragging it, you might display a menu that prevents you from dragging the image. Also, if you click a linked image or text, you will jump to the page the image or text is linked to.

Important: If you are using a Web browser (such as Navigator 3.0 for Windows or Explorer 3.0 for MacOS) that does not support dragging and dropping of objects from the browser window to the PageMill window, you'll need to skip steps 4 and 5 and place the object manually in PageMill. To do that, click an insertion point just before the "C" in "Click here to download the Adobe Acrobat Reader." Then click the Place Object button in the toolbar, locate the Images folder in the Lesson9 folder, and double-click the ACROBUT.GIF file. After placing the button, skip to step 6.

4 Position the pointer over the Get Acrobat Reader button, but don't click.

5 Using a swift and smooth motion (clicking but not releasing the mouse button), drag the button from the Adobe home page to the EVENTS.HTM window, just in front of the line "Click here to download the Adobe Acrobat Reader."

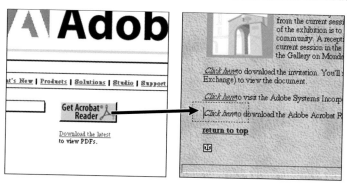

Now you'll create the link with an absolute URL.

6 Drag to select the button you just added and the text "Click here" in the line "Click here to download the Adobe Acrobat Reader."

7 Go back to the Adobe home page and find the linked text "Download the latest" near the Get Acrobat Reader button.

8 Using the same smooth motion as in step 5, drag the linked text from the Adobe home page onto the selected text and button on the Events page. The "Click here" text and border around the button should change to the reddish-brown color you defined for links in Lesson 2.

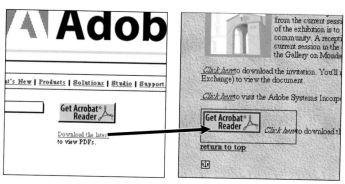

If the link appears as text outside the button, choose Edit Undo (Windows) or Edit Undo Create Link (MacOS). Then make sure the button and "Click here" text are selected and drag the link again.

If you cannot drag and drop the link at all, try typing the address in the Link To bar at the bottom of the EVENTS.HTM window. You must type the address exactly as shown in lowercase letters. Remember to press Enter or Return when you finish typing. In the Link To bar, type:

http://www.adobe.com/acrobat/readstep.html

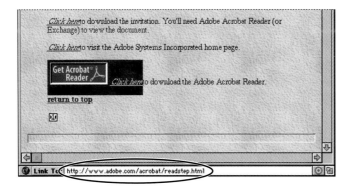

The URL for the Acrobat Reader is added to the link and is displayed in the Link To text box at the bottom of the EVENTS.HTM window.

When visitors to the Art Academy Web site click this link, they'll be led through the process of downloading the correct version of the Acrobat Reader software for their platform. Once again, you can quickly test the external link.

9 In PageMill, choose File > Save Page.

10 Click the Edit icon to switch to Preview mode.

11 Click the link you just created.

In the Web browser, a page in the Adobe Web site opens, describing how to download the Acrobat Reader application.

12 Close the Web browser window.

Using other URL types

An absolute URL does not have to begin with http. You can include other URL types supported by Web browsers, such as ftp, gopher, and mailto. PageMill supports the following URL types:

file:// Opens a file on a currently available disk or folder.

http:// Opens a World Wide Web page.

ftp:// Connects to a server using the File Transfer Protocol, allowing you to browse and download files on the server.

gopher:// Connects to a Gopher server.

telnet:// Connects to a server using Telnet, which lets you log on to the server.

news: Connects to a Usenet newsgroup.

mailto: Sends an electronic mail message.

snews: Opens a secure newsgroup connection.

shttp:// Opens a secure World Wide Web connection.

In this procedure, you'll use one of the handiest URLs—the "mailto" URL which lets visitors to a Web site send electronic mail (e-mail).

The Art Academy Web site includes a mail address on the home page. You'll go there now to establish the link.

1 In PageMill, choose File > Open and double-click the HOME.HTM file in the Lesson9 folder.

2 In the HOME.HTM window, click the Preview icon to switch to Edit mode.

3 Scroll, if necessary, to view the footer section, then select the text "Webmaster@artacad.edu" in the last line.

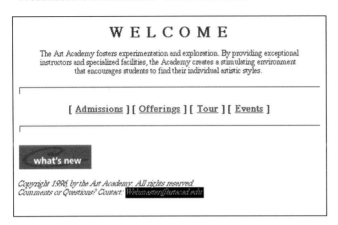

You'll make this address become the source of the mail.

Note: The source of a "mailto" link does not have to be a mail address—for example, the text might read "Click here to send mail."

4 Since creating the "mailto" link requires that you specify an e-mail address, choose Edit > Copy. This way you'll avoid having to retype it.

5 In the Link To bar at the bottom of the window, type **mailto:** and then choose Edit > Paste. Press Enter or Return.

6 Choose File > Save Page.

If you are able to upload your site to a Web server during this lesson, and your Web browser is properly configured to send mail, you can test this link by replacing "Webmaster@artacad.edu" with an actual e-mail address, such as your own. Be sure to leave the "mailto:" part of the URL.

If you cannot upload the Web pages you create in this lesson, and only use your browser to open the Web site files locally, you can still see how the browser lets you type a mail message when you click this link.

7 Choose View > Switch To (Windows) or Window > Switch To (MacOS), then choose a Web browser.

The Web browser displays the Home page.

8 Scroll down the page to the footer and click the e-mail address you linked to earlier in the procedure.

If the browser is properly configured for electronic mail, the Mail window appears. (Otherwise, the browser may prompt you to specify mail preferences; if so, cancel the prompt and skip step 9.)

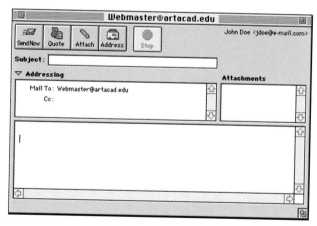

The message is automatically set to go to the mail address you typed in the Link To bar.

Because your pages have not been uploaded to a Web server and so are not connected to the Internet, any mail you send at this point will not actually reach its destination.

9 Close the Mail window.

Linking to movies

You'll complete this final lesson by including links to a QuickTime movie and an animated GIF file. You've created links to files in several different ways. Another way to create a link is to drag a file from a folder onto a selected image or text.

MacOS note: *Before you can play a QuickTime movie in a browser, you must flatten the movie. You can flatten movies using any version of Adobe Premiere®, or other applications such as MoviePlayer 2.0, Movie Converter 1.0, or FlattenMooV. For instructions on flattening movies, see your application's documentation.*

1 Open the EVENTS.HTM window, then click the "Open House" link to go to the "20-Year Anniversary Open House" section.

2 Click the Preview icon to switch to Edit mode.

3 Select the filmstrip image in this section.

4 Locate the file MOVIE.MOV in the Lesson9 folder, then drag it on top of the selected image to create the link.

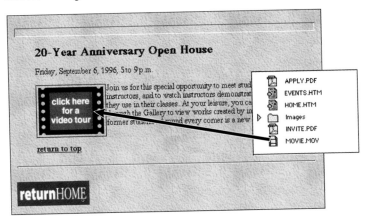

5 In PageMill, choose View > Show Inspector (Windows) or Window > Show Inspector (MacOS).

6 Type 1 for Border and press Enter or Return.

7 Choose File > Save Page.

Now you can test the movie link from a Web browser.

In Windows, you can test the movie link from within PageMill. Simply click the Edit icon to switch to Preview mode. Click the image labeled "Click here for a video tour," then click the forward arrow on the left side of the playbar to start the movie.

8 Choose View > Switch To (Windows) or Window > Switch To (MacOS), then choose a Web browser.

9 Once again, click the "Open House" link at the top of the page to go to the "20-Year Anniversary Open House" section.

10 Click the image labeled "Click here for a video tour."

As the browser downloads the movie, an icon is displayed in the center of the window. When the browser has finished downloading the movie, the movie's poster frame—the frame that appears when the movie is not playing—appears in the browser window.

11 Click the forward arrow on the left side of the playbar to start the movie.

12 When you finish watching the movie, quit the Web browser.

Note: You can also embed a flattened movie in a PageMill page by dragging the movie file from a folder, the Desktop, or the PageMill pasteboard. For more information, see Chapter 4, "Adding Movies, Images, and Sounds" in the Adobe PageMill 2.0 User Guide.

Linking to an animated GIF file

Finally, you'll create a link to an animated GIF file. An animated GIF file is a simple form of animation that quickly plays a sequence of images one after another to produce the illusion of movement. The effect is similar to flipping the pages of a book that contain figures drawn in different positions.

You can create an animated GIF file by using a shareware program called GifBuilder to assemble two or more images. For more information about GifBuilder, see the following page on the Adobe Web site:

http://www.adobe.com/studio/tipstechniques/GIFanimation/main.html

Once you create the animated GIF file, you can place it on a Web page as you would place any other GIF file. Once placed, the animation automatically plays according to the options you specified in GifBuilder.

You'll place a completed animated GIF file on the Events page.

1 In the EVENTS.HTM window, scroll up, if necessary, to the heading "Lecture Series," then click an insertion point before the word "This" in the first paragraph.

2 Click the Place Object button (▣) in the toolbar, locate and open the Images folder in the Lesson9 folder, then double-click the ANIMATED.GIF file.

3 Select the image, then click the Right Align Object button (▣≣) in the upper right area of the toolbar.

In Windows only, the right side of the toolbar may be hidden, depending on the size of the PageMill window. To view the entire toolbar, you may have to enlarge the PageMill window, then maximize the EVENTS.HTM window.

4 Click the Edit icon to switch to Preview mode.

PageMill automatically plays the animation. To stop it from playing, click the image. To start the animation again, double-click the image.

Congratulations on completing the last lesson. Have fun creating your own Web site!

Review questions

1 What type of URL would you specify when linking to a file on another disk, folder, or server and why?

2 Why is using PDF on the Web better than HTML for design-intensive documents?

3 When do you use the "mailto" URL type?

4 How can you add simple animation to a Web page?

Answers

1 You would specify an absolute URL, which includes the complete and unique location of a file on a network.

2 PDF preserves the design of the document, including fonts, layout, and color.

3 The "mailto" URL type sends electronic mail messages.

4 You can place an animated GIF image on the Web page.

Web Basics

The Internet's World Wide Web (the Web) is an increasingly popular medium for distributing and viewing information in the form of pages of text and images. This section introduces Web concepts and terminology, and offers tips for creating and uploading a Web site. For more information about Web concepts and building Web sites, see Chapter 2, "Basic Concepts" in the *Adobe PageMill 2.0 User Guide*. For a comprehensive list of Internet and Web terms, see the glossary in the next section.

What is a Web site?

On the Web, a *site* is a group of related pages that reside together on a Web server. When you edit your Web site on your computer with Adobe PageMill, your site exists as a group of Web pages inside a folder on a hard disk attached to your computer. The site folder can contain images and subfolders containing more folders, images, and Web pages.

You can prepare and maintain a site on a computer away from the Web server, such as on your home computer or laptop, and then *upload*, or send a copy of, the site to the Web server where it will be published electronically to the world.

Creating Web pages visually

Every page on the Web is described using the Hypertext Markup Language (HTML). Many other applications for designing Web pages require you to learn the actual HTML codes that format the text and graphics on a page. PageMill lets you create pages without typing any codes. You can format text by choosing formats from menus, and you can import, resize, and reposition graphics on the page simply by dragging them.

If you want to, you can enter custom HTML code into Adobe PageMill when, for example, you want to add a feature or special effect not directly supported by this version of PageMill, such as blinking text.

Understanding Web page design issues

Your options for page design are much different for a Web page than for the printed page. If you're new to designing Web pages, you'll need to get to know the capabilities of HTML. Even though you do not have to enter HTML code to create a Web page, the capabilities of HTML determine what you are able to present on a Web page.

Depending on the kind of pages you want to design, HTML may expand or limit your design options. The following overview is of the differences between designing for the printed page and for a Web page. For design tips and more information on electronic publishing, see the online Adobe magazine at **http://www.adobemag.com/**.

Layout considerations and restrictions with HTML

HTML is primarily a set of tags for a sequence of text and images, with hypertext links; it is not a page-layout language like Adobe PageMaker®. For your Web page to achieve the same effect on the Web as a PageMaker page on paper, you would need to save files in the Adobe Acrobat Portable Document Format (PDF). In HTML, you can achieve a similar effect using tables and setting the borders to 0.

In HTML, you cannot control the size of the page and the width of the text column, because the page proportions and line breaks can vary, depending on the size of the monitor or window in which the page is viewed, and with the size of the font the reader chooses in a Web browser. However, as a rough guideline, you might design for the line length produced by a Web browser using a default font on a 640x480-pixel screen. Also, a Web browser on a computer running Windows tends to display fonts larger than a browser on a computer running MacOS.

 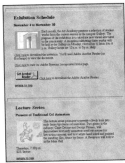 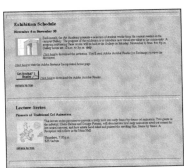

Page proportions and line breaks can vary, depending on the size of the monitor or window.

Because images are part of the text stream in HTML, you cannot specify a precise horizontal and vertical position for an image. For example, if you position an image at the bottom right of a page as it appears on your monitor and a reader decides to make the window narrower, the image will probably move to the next line down and may end up on the left side of the page. To work around these limitations, you can use borderless tables to position text, images, and other multimedia and plug-in objects.

Typographical considerations

You cannot set type specifications that affect typographical density using HTML, because line breaks, letter spacing, and word spacing are completely determined by the size of the window and the font settings in a Web browser. In addition, the following type characteristics are either completely controlled or not supported by Web browsers and cannot be specified from within Adobe PageMill or imported from other applications:

- Font, type size, and leading.

- Font width

- Tracking

- Strikethrough, outline, shadow, reverse, superscript, and subscript type styles

- Tab positions

- Spacing before or after a paragraph

If you want to preserve the typography in a short passage of text, such as a company logo, create the text in an image-processing program, such as Adobe Photoshop, and import it as an image. However, text saved as an image takes much longer to download than plain text.

Structuring a page around HTML formats

Although the constraints of HTML may seem to be limitations from the point of view of a printed-page designer, they are intended as advantages for online delivery. The goal of HTML is to make Web pages readable on a wide variety of computer systems and monitor sizes. The HTML approach to this goal specifies the informational structure of a page separately from its appearance. The page author creates the structure, and the reader specifies the appearance.

HTML structures information using named formats. You apply formats based on the function of a particular piece of text, such as a heading, a regular paragraph, or a list. HTML formats are similar to the named styles in many word-processing programs in that the author can change the appearance of text by applying them. However, the appearance of a format might also be changed by a person reading a Web page with a browser, something a reader of a printed page cannot do. The formats in HTML are built so that the functional organization of the page is preserved even if a reader changes the appearance of a format.

Preserving a graphical layout on the Web

If preserving a sophisticated graphic identity or page layout is important, consider creating some of your Web pages as PDF files. PDF files preserve the layout and typographical characteristics that are not preserved by HTML, and can include hypertext links between pages and to the Web.

PDF files preserve layout and typography.

Adobe PageMill lets you include PDF files in your Web site and manage links from HTML files to them. If you include PDF files, you should provide a link to the free Adobe Acrobat Reader application, required to view PDF files. Acrobat Reader can be configured as a helper application for browsers, interpreting the PDF format for browsers that do not support it directly. Acrobat Reader runs on computers running MacOS, Windows, MS-DOS®, and some UNIX systems. For more information about PDF files and Adobe Acrobat, see the Adobe Web site at **http://www.adobe.com**.

Web links

Links are one of the most significant differences between printed pages and Web pages. Web pages can contain hypertext links to other Web pages or to other parts of the same page. When you click a link, the Web browser takes you to the page set as a destination for the link. Links appear as specially marked text or images on the page. In Adobe PageMill, creating a link can be as simple as dragging the icon of a page onto selected text or an image.

When you design a Web site, links let you create nonsequential arrangements of pages. Instead of having one page follow another as in a printed book, several links may be sprinkled throughout each page, with each link leading directly to another page containing links to even more pages. You can link pages into the most appropriate structure for the information you are conveying.

Links can lead to other pages within your site or to pages on any other Web server in the world, giving your readers access to additional information related to the content you are presenting. A diagram of the complex link structures that exist on the Web today would in fact resemble a net or web across the world.

Building a Web site

As with any publishing project, planning is important and can save you much time and trouble later. A Web site is structured very differently from printed books and periodicals, and is dependent on both local and network hardware and software.

For information on creating a Web site, see "Building a Web site" in chapter 2 of the *Adobe PageMill 2.0 User Guide.* In addition, use the following tips to avoid common problems when constructing a Web site. Many of these tips come directly from the Adobe Web site's Technical Solutions Database at **http://www.adobe.com/support service/custsupport/tssearchdb.html.**

To maintain links in your site, you can use Adobe SiteMill™, a site-management program for the Web. SiteMill works hand in hand with PageMill by automatically maintaining correct links throughout a Web site even as it grows and changes. For information about SiteMill, see the Adobe Web site at **http://www.adobe.com/.**

Talking to your Internet Service Provider (ISP)

Before creating your Web site, ask your ISP the following questions:

1 Is the Web server running on a UNIX workstation, a DOS computer, or a MacOS computer?

2 What is the path to the root directory of your Web site on the server? (This is important if you are creating server-side image maps.)

3 Does your ISP make any CGI (Common Gateway Interface) scripts available to subscribers? CGI scripts are necessary to implement image maps and forms on most Web servers. Obtain instructions from your ISP to use CGI scripts successfully.

4 Which image map file format does the Web server use, client-side or server-side?

5 What is the correct procedure to use when you are ready to upload your Web site to the server? Many ISPs have specific rules that govern how files are uploaded to the server.

Setting up PageMill preferences

With the answers your ISP provides, you can correctly set up PageMill preferences. Customizing preference options before creating your Web site ensures that your site's links will work as expected when the site is uploaded to a Web server.

To customize preferences in PageMill, see "Setting PageMill Preferences" on page 5 of this Classroom in a Book.

If you are creating server-side image maps, you need to specify the map format and server location preferences. For information on setting those preferences, see Chapter 6, "Creating Image Maps" in the *Adobe PageMill 2.0 User Guide.*

Creating a mirror folder

Web pages include links to external files, rather than the contents of external files. To ensure links in your Web site remain valid, you must preserve your file's relative positions after you create links. You can preserve relative file positions by creating and using a pair of mirrored site folders, one on the local hard disk, and one on the Web server. When you initially upload your local site folder to the Web server, both folders should be identical. Any changes you make to the local folder need to be made to the site folder to preserve the mirror relationship.

If you are unable to upload your entire site folder at the same time, create a folder structure on the Web server that matches the folder structure of your local site folder, then upload the site files into the appropriate folders.

Naming your Web pages

Web pages need a filename extension appropriate to the platform from which you publish them. If your Web server is a DOS computer, use .HTM. If your Web server is a MacOS computer or UNIX workstation, use .HTML. Files without filename extensions display the HTML code of the Web page, rather than the formatted page.

Use alphanumeric characters when you are naming Web pages. For the maximum compatibility with all computers, use eight-character, single-word filenames, such as document.html. If you must use more than one word when you name Web pages, use an underscore (_) or hyphen (-) rather than a space character. Space characters become ASCII-encoded, and links to the file are broken.

Many Web servers are case sensitive. When you create links manually, make sure you match the case of the file to which you are linking.

Locating and naming your image files

PageMill and SiteMill can import images in GIF, JPEG, and PICT format. When importing PICT images, PageMill and SiteMill convert the PICT image into a GIF image, and store the GIF image file in the Resource folder. To specify a default resource folder, choose Edit > Preferences and select a folder within your local site folder. Then place the images you wish to use into this folder before inserting them into your Web pages.

PageMill and SiteMill name converted PICT files using this format: image1.gif, image2.gif, image3.gif, in numeric order. If you want more control over the names of image files within your Web site, convert PICT files to either GIF or JPEG format before you import them.

Image files need a filename extension appropriate to the platform from which you publish them. If your Web server is a DOS computer, use .GIF or .JPG. If your Web server is a MacOS computer or UNIX workstation, use .GIF or .JPEG.

Files without filename extensions display the code of the image file in a Web browser, rather than the image.

Use alphanumeric characters when you name image files, and for the greatest compatibility use eight-character, single-word filenames, such as photo.gif. If you must use more than one word when you name image files, use an underscore (_) or hyphen (-) rather than a space character. Space characters become ASCII-encoded, and links to the file are broken.

Uploading your Web site

When you upload your Web site to the server, send HTML files as text, and all other files as raw data. If you upload files using a different format, links will not work as expected, and graphics will not display.

If you upload your Web site using a standard FTP utility, such as Dartmouth Fetch, refer to support documentation for answers to questions and contact your ISP for support. For more information on uploading files and using Fetch, see Chapter 10, "Uploading Your Web Site" in the *Adobe PageMill 2.0 User Guide*.

Test the pages by connecting to them from the Web server. If everything works, your pages are now available to anyone in the world with a connected Web browser.

Glossary

absolute URL A complete pathname to the location of a file on a **network**, starting with the root of the **Web server** on which the file resides, then listing any folders or directories, and ending with the name of the file. For example, a **Web page** could have an absolute **URL** such as:

http://www.adobe.com/supportservice/custsupport/main.html

To maintain the **hyperlink** to the absolute URL, the file must remain in the same directory on the same server. If the file is moved, the URL will no longer match the directory names in the path.

address The location of a computer, file, or other object on a **network**, as in **FTP** address. See also **URL**.

Adobe Acrobat The universal electronic publishing tool from Adobe Systems, Inc. for distributing documents on the Web, corporate intranets, e-mail, Lotus Notes®, network file servers, CD-ROM, or print-on-demand systems. Acrobat converts electronic files to Adobe Portable Document Format (PDF), which preserves color, graphics, fonts, formatting, and links to the Web.

anchor The destination page, file, or object in a **hyperlink**. See also **source**.

anti-aliasing Blending colors to provide a smoother, softer edge to on-screen fonts.

applet A small, platform-independent program written in the Java programming language that executes within an HTML document displayed by a Web browser. These mini-applications can be used for animation, interactive forms, sounds, etc.

backbone High-speed, long-distance **networks** that are the foundation of the **Internet**.

bandwidth The amount of data that can be carried through a phone line at one time.

bookmark A **Web browser** feature that lets you make a record of a **Web page** and its address so you can find it again easily.

browser See **Web browser**.

CGI (Common Gateway Interface) A language that allows communication between a **Web browser** and a **Web server** for processing **image maps** and forms, for responding to search requests, and so on.

client A computer that just receives information from a server. See also **host**.

client-side image map An image map that stores hot spot coordinates and links directly within the HTML page, not in a separate map-definition file, as do **server-side image maps**. Client-side image maps display linked pages faster because the maps are processed by the **Web browser** used to view the **Web page**. Not all Web browsers support client-side image maps. (Netscape Navigator 2.0 and later and Microsoft Internet Explorer do.) See also **server-side image map**.

content Text, images, animation, movies, and sounds available on the Internet.

domain The unique name of a specific network on the **Internet**. The domain name is part of a **URL** and is also used for e-mail. For example, in the URL http://www.adobe.com, www.adobe.com is the domain name.

download To receive a file (such as programs, text, images, animation, movies, or sounds) from a **host** computer.

FAQ (Frequently Asked Questions) Often a separate section within a **Web site** that answer the most common questions on a particular topic.

firewall Security software and procedures that protect a system from unauthorized use.

frames A set of **HTML** code used to partition certain areas of the **Web page** for navigational aids and more.

FTP (File Transfer Protocol) A method for transferring data from one computer to another. Also the program that **downloads** or **uploads** files (such as programs, text, images, movies, or sounds) to or from a computer.

GIF (Graphics Interchange Format) A standard compression scheme for images, limited to 8-bit or 256 colors. GIF is best for text, line art, or images with large, adjacent, solid colors.

hit A request from a computer on the Internet for a particular file on a **Web site**.

home page The first page you see on a **Web page** or the top level of information at a particular site.

host A single or multiuser computer that can send and receive data over the **Internet**. See also **Web server**.

hot spots Areas on an **image map** that jump to other locations on the **Web**.

HTML (Hypertext Mark-Up Language) A set of codes used to define the behavior of text, graphics, and other elements on a **Web page.**

HTTP (Hypertext Transport Protocol) A specific method or set of instructions for transferring data between a Web **browser** and a **Web server.**

hyperlink A specially marked portion of a **Web page**—a single word, a sentence, or an image—that takes you to another Web page when clicked. See also **hypertext** and **URL.**

hypertext Specially marked text that links **Web pages** together. See also **URL.**

image map A single image that contains multiple links to **URLs.** Clicking different parts of the image, called **hot spots,** activates different links and displays the URL that corresponds to that part of the image. See also **client-side image map** and **server-side image map.**

interlaced GIF An image that is displayed by the Web browser with increasing amounts of information rather than after all the image data has been transmitted. The browser builds the image by displaying a grainy version first, then successively filling in the details until a full-resolution version appears.

Internet A network of millions of networked computers worldwide that carries services such as e-mail and the **Web.** (Also Cyberspace, the Net, Infobahn, and Information Highway). Started in 1969 by the Department of Defense for military purposes, the Internet now connects about 40 million higher-education, government, military, and commercial users.

Intranet A private company's in-house computer network that uses **Internet** standards and technology. The Intranet may have its own **Web server** and public and private mail systems.

IP (Internet Protocol) A low-level method or set of instructions for transferring information on the **Internet.**

ISDN (Integrated Services Digital Network) A type of high-capacity phone line for digital transmission of text, graphics, audio, and video. ISDN is designed to carry 128K bits per second one way, or 256K bits per second simultaneously.

ISP (Internet Service Provider) A private company that provides access to the **Internet** to commercial and private users. ISPs also provide space for storing your own **Web pages.**

Java A computer programming language developed by Sun Microsystems that works with HTML to allow dynamic programs to run and interact with a computer. Java enables the creation of **applets** that execute in response to mouse clicks and produce sound, video, or other effects within a **Web browser.**

JPEG (Joint Photographic Experts Group) A standard compression scheme for images. JPEG is best for photographic images or images with gradients. JPEG images cannot be made transparent or interlaced.

link See **hyperlink**.

modem A device that takes digital information and converts it to electrical pulses that can be sent over a telephone line and, conversely, takes these impulses and changes them to digital data.

page See **Web page**.

pathname In Unix and DOS operating systems, the literal path from the topmost directory of a disk to a file.

PDF See **Adobe Acrobat**.

plug-in A software component that adds a new feature to a specific program.

protocol A set of rules that describes how information is transferred on the Internet. The method used by the Web to transfer information is called HTTP (Hypertext Transfer Protocol).

relative URL The location of the linked **Web page** relative to the current page. In the following example, the two periods tell the **Web browser** that the file is located in the folder above the folder containing the current page.

../main.html

If a file referenced by a relative **URL** is moved to another directory or **Web server,** or if the folder name changes, the **hyperlink** continues to work as long as the file exists one directory up in the hierarchy.

router A machine on the **Internet** that examines every packet of data that passes through it and directs it toward its destination.

server-side image map An **image map** that requires two files: an HTML file that contains an image and a separate map-definition file for the link, stored on the **Web server**. Server-side maps are slower than **client-side image maps** because they are processed on the **Web server** by the server software. However, unlike client-side maps, server-side maps are supported by most **Web browsers**.

site See **Web site**.

source The text or object that jumps to an **anchor** in a **hyperlink**.

TCP/IP (Transmission Control Protocol/Internet Protocol) A series of instruction sets that other programs must adhere to, thus ensuring consistent and reliable operation on the **backbone** of the **Internet**.

upload To send a copy of a file (graphics file, **PDF** document, application, and so on) to a **Web server** where others can access it.

URL (Uniform Resource Locator) An address to a specific file or location on the Web that all browsers recognize. A URL always begins with an Internet **protocol**, then includes the **domain**, intermediary directories or folders within the file structure of the Web site, and ends with the filename of the **Web page**. See also **absolute URL** and **relative URL**.

Web (World Wide Web) A subset of the **Internet** that uses images, multimedia elements, and **hypertext** navigation to communicate information globally.

Web browser A program that enables users to interact with a **Web server and** see **Web pages**. Sometimes called "client software." Each browser interprets the HTML code differently and, therefore, displays the **Web page** differently.

Webmaster Someone who creates **Web pages** and manages a **Web server**.

Web page A document of any length on a **Web server**. The page can contain text, images, animation, movies, and sounds that are displayed on your screen by a **Web browser**.

Web server The computer that physically holds the **Web site** on its hard disk and transfers **Web pages** and information over the **Internet** as they are requested using one or more standard **protocols**, such as HTTP, FTP, and so on.

Web site A collection of related **Web pages** on a **Web server**. You usually enter a Web site via a **home page**.

Index